# #WhyAm...

## BECAUSE...

# Relationships!

### The 5 essentials you need to successfully maintain ALL of the relationships in your life

*(without yelling)*

## KRISTA RIZZO, CPC

Publisher's Note: This is a work of nonfiction. Names, characters, places, and incidents are a product of the author's personal experience.

Why Am I Yelling? LLC

Ebook: 978-1-7328572-0-9

Print: 978-1-7328572-2-3

*For Sweet William*

*ILY*

# What's In This Book

Because...*Why* Am *I Yelling?*. . . . . . . . . . . . . . . . . . . . . . . . 1

The 5 Essentials. . . . . . . . . . . . . . . . . . . . . . . . . . . . . . . . 7

## Part 1: Relationships With Yourself

Because...*Self Love!* . . . . . . . . . . . . . . . . . . . . . . . . . . . . 19

Because...*Body Love!* . . . . . . . . . . . . . . . . . . . . . . . . . . . . 33

Because...*Mind Love!*. . . . . . . . . . . . . . . . . . . . . . . . . . . . 54

Because...*Spiritual Love!*. . . . . . . . . . . . . . . . . . . . . . . . . 66

## Part 2: Relationships With Others

Because...*Relationships & Growing Up!* . . . . . . . . . . . . . . 89

Because...*The One!*. . . . . . . . . . . . . . . . . . . . . . . . . . . . . 144

Because...*Building a Family!*. . . . . . . . . . . . . . . . . . . . . . 158

Because...*Friendships!*. . . . . . . . . . . . . . . . . . . . . . . . . . . . 176

Because...*The Death of a Relationship!*. . . . . . . . . . . . . . . 196

Because...*What I Know* . . . . . . . . . . . . . . . . . . . . . . . . . 203

Acknowledgements . . . . . . . . . . . . . . . . . . . . . . . . . . . . 205

## BECAUSE...

# Why AM I Yelling?!

I get that question all the time. People want to know how in the hell I came up with the name — Why Am I Yelling? for my blog and now, everything I do in my business. Well, I'll tell ya. In May of 2010, I was on a trip with two of my girlfriends in Spain. (I know, tough life, but *someone's* gotta do it!) One afternoon after a day of sightseeing, we were sitting by the pool at our villa, sipping cocktails and chatting about life. One of my friends posed the question, "If you could have any job in the world, what would you do?" Without hesitation I answered, "I would be a talk show host."

My response was met with enthusiasm and comments like, "Oh, you would be an awesome talk show host!" or "That suits you to a tee." Fast forward a few weeks later, and I got an email from one of the girls from the trip. It included a link to enter a contest that was being sponsored by Oprah Winfrey. The name of the contest was "Your Own Show" and Oprah was looking for the next up-and-coming talk show host. The prize was getting the opportunity to have your talk show idea come to life. My friends were adamant that I enter the contest. Although it was several weeks in, I decided what the heck, and we created the requisite video for submission.

While planning to do the video, I had to come up with a name and an idea. I have no idea why but, *Why Am I Yelling?* popped into my brain and I couldn't stop thinking about it. So, I created a show around that name. My talk show would not be your typical show that was dotted with celebrities talking about their latest projects or touting their wares. I wanted it to be different. I felt like we had enough of those shows, so let's try something new. My show was going to be me traveling around the world, meeting with real life people, talking about real life. We would be "yelling" about all the things worth a voice-raising — good, bad, happy or sad.

The reason I chose the word *yelling* is because for me, it means passion. We yell for so many reasons. Yes, when we're frustrated or mad (that's what first comes to mind usually), but if you think about it, we use our ability to raise our voices in a bunch of ways. We yell with excitement when we're cheering at a sporting event, singing along at a concert, or celebrating a significant life milestone. I know we tend to associate yelling with bad things, but for me it's about being passionate about life and yelling about all of it. It's meant to be cheeky, fun and energetic.

So, I entered the contest. We made a two-minute video, submitted it and got around a hundred thousand votes in three weeks. Not too shabby for a late entry, but not enough to be a finalist. During the process I decided to document my progress by writing a blog with the same name. And that, my friends is how *Why*

*Am I Yelling?* was born. Eight years, and a lot of blog posts later, it's the name of my business, my hashtag and my brand. It just made sense for me to keep it alive. It's my personality. It's bold and fearless. It's playful and loud, and I'm pretty sure if you ask someone who knows me well, they will use one of those words to describe me.

I've been a professional coach for years. I love it. I love helping others change their lives, realize their dreams and transform into the people they've envisioned becoming. I love learning about relationships and guiding through career transitions. I love getting to know new people and inspiring them to reach for the stars and beyond.

The road I had initially carved out to lead me to my own success has twisted and turned in unexpected directions, one of which is this book. I mean, I've had an idea to write a book for a while, I just didn't think it would happen so quickly in my profession. Yet, here I am, pouring my heart out by sharing my personal and vulnerable stories in the hopes that it will inspire you to realize that you have the power to change your life and your relationships. That you hold the key to your happiness. That you *deserve* to have everything you've ever dreamed of, if you do the work and make the commitment to making it happen.

I was encouraged to write this book by my husband who works in the news business. I am a contributor to the *Today Show Parenting* website. Last year, one of my articles was retweeted by a colleague of my husband's. When I told him, he acknowledged that he knew the person who retweeted my piece. I said something like, "How do I get to be on the *Today Show* couch?" His response was matter of fact, as he was getting dressed to go to work. He said "Write the book." So, I said, "Ok, I'll write the book." *Today Show*, here I come! Conversation over. Lemme run and get my pencil...

It's easy to decide to write a book. It's hard to actually write one. I vacillated for a while about the topic. I knew I wanted to create a *#WhyAmIYelling?* series, but wasn't sure where to begin. Which book should be first? How many did I want to write? Will I offend anyone? Should I care? Will people like them? All these questions were hindering my process to begin, or perhaps I was stalling? I don't know.

Then one day, in the summer of 2016, I was so inspired by my son, Wyatt that I finally, and without a doubt, had to start writing this book. He was ten years old at the time, and about to enter middle school in Brooklyn, NY. When you have a kid in the NYC school system going to middle school, they typically take city transportation to school. Yellow school buses are not provided for them, Metrocards are. My husband and I decided he would need to have a cellphone since he would be navigating the streets alone and so in July we decided to give him a phone. Ground rules were created. We made it very clear that his new-found obsession would be heavily monitored and that he could not have access to certain apps. His social media, which was and still is pretty non-existent, would also be made available to us whenever we asked. He balked at none of it.

What was most interesting was watching the way the interaction with his friends changed as soon as the devices showed up. Dynamics changed between the boys and the girls. Relationships were blossoming, and maturing right before our eyes. I felt the pull to write the story I was watching unfold. (You'll hear more about this story with Wyatt later in the book!)

It was then that I decided the first book in the "#WhyAmIYelling?" series would be about relationships, and of course, communication.

I wanted this book to be different than a typical relationship book. I'm not here to tell you what you are doing wrong. I'm going to show you my experiences bumping around through relationships so that you can see what success, and failure, look like. And, because communication is the make or break of every relationship, that's what we're gonna be talking about here — in every type of relationship. There are so many books out there that focus on specific types of relationships. Some on romance or marriage. Other books for parents and children. I wanted to touch on all kinds of relationships, or at least the ones that I've encountered in my life.

I decided to write this book from all of the relationship perspectives I have available to me, as a woman, daughter, friend and mother because each one shows the different ways we relate and communicate with one another. I want to share my loving and bumpy life experiences and how they shaped the person I've become. I hope you will find yourself in these stories as I did. Here are some of the questions I asked myself as I prepared to write this book, I'm keeping them in here so you can see how I started.

How were you introduced to your relationships?

What would you change?

How have you changed the way you were taught versus the way you cultivate your relationships now?

Interesting to think about, right?

In the pages of this book, my hope is that you resonate with my stories. That you're reminded of times in your life where you had similar feelings. My hope is that you realize the importance of every relationship in your life — most importantly the one you have with yourself. I hope you're inspired and entertained as you read. And I hope you keep the relationship essentials that I talk about in the back of your mind as you do.

Writing these stories has been a journey for me. It's opened the floodgates of memories, good, bad and everything in between. It's helped me gain closure in some cases, and realize mistakes I've made in others. It is my honor to share my journey, and their lessons with you. Thank you for reading these words. I appreciate you.

# The 5 Essentials

I've done a lot of work and research in the relationship area, and while I haven't found the book that encompasses all relationships, like this one does, they all have a theme. The marriage books talk about communication, intimacy and respect. The parenting books talk about everything from boundaries and discipline to emotions and problem resolution. The self-love books talk about topics like forgiveness and self-esteem.

When I was outlining this book, I realized that since a book like this one doesn't really exist, I wanted to highlight the most important elements in every relationship we have. So, I created my list of these important parts and I call it, The 5 Essentials of Successful Relationships. Now, of course there are more, but if I included all of them, this book would be a million pages long and get off track quickly. I polled some friends and clients and asked where they struggled most in relationship, and this is the list that won out over all.

## The 5 Essentials of Successful Relationships

Communication
Intimacy
Boundaries
Respect
Support

So waddaya think? Ya feeling me on these? I mean, it seems pretty obvious, truth be told, yet sometimes we can lose touch with one or two of these Essentials as we navigate the relationships in our lives. It's easy to do if we're not paying attention and focusing on what's really important. And at the end of the day the most important thing is that we are all feeling good about the relationships we're building, nurturing and experiencing. So, here's a little summary of each of the Essentials. As we move through this book you'll see how they fit into every relationship we have throughout our lives.

## BECAUSE... *You've Got to Communicate!*

I'll say it multiple times throughout this book, and I'll say it until I'm blue in the face: communication is the single most important element in EVERY relationship you have. If you can't voice your thoughts or needs, good or bad, to the person you're having the thoughts about, then how are you supposed to have an honest relationship? Whether it's your marriage, partnership, with your children, friends, or whoever. Being able to communicate with the other person is how your relationships will thrive.

Communication isn't all sunshine and rainbows. It can be hard and messy, but it's necessary to have successful relationships throughout your life. Especially when it comes to the kids. At some point in your life you're going to have to say things to your children that you never thought you would. Whether it be disciplining them, or explaining situations to them that you hadn't anticipated (it happens every day). Being a good communicator can make all the difference in the outcome of the conversation, and your relationship.

Yes, it's important to be able to use your voice, but it is equally important to be a good listener. That's not easy to master, the listening. So often we get caught up in our words, and getting them out, that we neglect to listen to the person we're communicating with. Take a full minute now, to just listen to the room around you. Get in the practice now.

Most people aren't born as great communicators — speaking or listening. I happen to know some bad listeners. It's very hard not to get frustrated during a conversation when someone isn't listening. I get that not everyone has these skills. It can take years of attention to master.

It's so easy to jump into a conversation and start speaking right away. Next time you're in a conversation, check yourself. Are you jumping into the conversation, not really listening to the other person, just waiting to get back to the part when it's your turn to talk again? Or are you able to listen and be present, without having to interject your opinion? Don't be hard on yourself if you feel like you aren't so great of a listener yet. Its learned by doing. Just try it out in any next conversation. You may find you want to talk. Try your hardest not to, and just listen. See what happens.

The other side of the coin when it comes to communicating is the verbal side. I love to talk. Oh yeah! And while that's all fine and good, being a great talker means you can effectively get your point across in your conversations. Are you a concise communicator or a someone who takes a while to make their point? Are you loud or soft spoken? Is it easy for you to have challenging conversations? There's not wrong answer to any of these questions by the way. I just want you to be aware of the way you are, and find a tone and style that works for you. Effective communication is important in every relationship because you have to be able to convey your ideas and opinions in a way that's understandable and digestible. Use words and phrases that are tailored to the company you're in. For example, you wouldn't use your higher education vernacular when speaking to your toddler right?

There's never a bad time to be a good communicator. Conversations are more fun when you can have great dialogue with your people. It means you're engaged and present and that's really the ultimate goal when it comes to relationships.

## BECAUSE... *Intimacy Feels Good!*

Who doesn't love to be loved? The sense of touch is comforting, exciting and heart-warming. Intimacy in all of its forms is something we should experience every day. Intimacy is SUPER important, and SUPER easy to drop like a hot potato. Let's face it, even in a platonic relationship, affection is important. I'm a toucher. I like to hug and have physical connections with everyone I know, and I like to receive physical affection in return.

I also know when it comes to sexual intimacy it can be easy to get wrapped up in other stuff, and put sex on the back burner. Especially after having kids, or being in a relationship for a while... DO NOT DO THAT!!! Find a way to make it happen!!

Yes, especially after you have kids, sex can be the very last thing you even want to do. I get it. But do it anyway. Get your pre-baby, adult human, routines back as soon as you can. Even when you don't want to get intimate, and you end up doing it anyway, I doubt you're gonna say it wasn't worth it. Even if its bad sex, it's still sex! Am I right? (wink wink).

Humans need intimacy. Women especially need it. We need to be touched and hugged, it's a form of appreciation to us. We need it from our partners, our friends and our kids. If you don't make your intimacy a priority, then you may end up regretting it. Remember, your kids, God willing, are going to leave your house. Your partner, God willing, isn't. Have the sex. Give the hugs. Spread the love. And, of course, don't forget to be responsible while doing it. (That's the mother in me preparing for the sex talk with my tweenager. Oy!)

# BECAUSE... *Boundaries Matter!*

Yes, intimacy and connection are essential, but the opposite is also true. Boundaries, and having a clear definition of what is okay, or not, for you in relationships is definitely one of the Essentials. Being clear about where your boundaries are, and being able to discuss them with the people in your life is key. I've recently been having conversations with several of my clients about how to create and set boundaries for themselves in their relationships, AND with their kids.

Boundaries are crucial for all of your relationships. Yes, all of them. Knowing your limits on what you will and will not tolerate for yourself is important in creating an optimistic attitude for yourself. Learning how to socialize your needs can feel scary, but necessary. This is where you are clear about the things you need, like and don't like in a relationship. If you're not doing this already. Try it. I dare ya. Discuss a need you have in a relationship with someone else. Do it lovingly. If you feel guilty, then likely you are doing it right.

We've seen a lot in the world lately about inappropriate behavior and how women are no longer tolerating what they thought they had to in order to be successful at work. Women are taking responsibility for their boundaries in a clear, and resounding way. I mean, part of my, "Why I left my job" story includes my being treated in a way that I was not going to tolerate. While it happened at the tail end of my tenure, it put a bad taste in my mouth for sure. I knew what I was willing to accept, and that behavior was not it. I was very clear about my boundaries. I told the appropriate people about the situation and I walked away from it. I was a much happier person from that day forward. I never once regretting my decision.

Boundaries are associated with following your gut. I recognized those feelings at an early age. When I was at a party, and someone would offer me something illicit, I would get a gut feeling immediately that it wasn't right for me. I knew deep down what my boundaries were around these situations. Like I tell my kids, "Nothing great happens after midnight," in preparation for their teenage years. Let's face it, I can't lock them in a closet until they're old and gray, but I can help them make good choices.

## BECAUSE... *Respect, Yo!*

Communication + boundaries leads to respect. You cannot have a relationship without respect. Period. I will say that until the day I die — along with all the other stuff I say! But you really can't. I've seen relationships drag on, to the point of abuse because one person is disrespectful to the other. It makes my skin crawl.

I have nothing kind to say about any type of disrespect, especially when it's to a person you're in a relationship with. Vile is a word that comes to mind. You guys, please be nice to one another — even if that's not what you experienced growing up. There is another way. No name calling. Be nice. Words hurt. You can't take them back no matter how much you apologize.

Will, (my husband) and I made a pact early on in our relationship, to never call each other names should a discussion get heated. We're excellent at walking out of a room to collect thoughts, and return with the words we need to use to get our points across, but we don't call one another names. Ever. It makes so much sense. If you can't respect the person you've chosen to spend your life with, well then, my friend, there's a problem. You may not even know you're doing it, so pay attention, especially when you are reacting to someone else. Be aware of the words you use, of the actions you take. Kindness and respect can, and do, shift relationships. They are game-changers.

## BECAUSE... *Support Is Essential*

Finally my loves, a key piece of relationship success is to support and encourage one another. The biggest thing I've learned from my journey in the last few years after leaving my comfortable, dependable job and jumping without a parachute into creating my own path is that I could never have done it without the support of my husband and children. I'm sure there have been and and still are times when Will has looked at me and thought I'm crazy for doing this. I'm sure he's muttered to himself that it would be easier if I just got another job and we weren't in a constant state of flux. But then I'll get an out of the blue note from him or we'll have a conversation that ends with him saying "you have to do this" and I know. I know that he has my back.

We may not approve of a decision other people make in their lives, but before we step into judgement, or fly off the handle, how about we take a step back and try to understand it from their perspective? How about we try to figure out how to engage one another and work through the issue together? Support and encourage one another. Great things happen when you do.

Those are my relationship musts. My clients, friends, neighbors, fellow parents, anyone I speak to really hears about these 5 Essentials all the time. They are now a part of your life too. Let's talk about how to use them in ALL of the relationships you have. We're gonna start with the most important relationship in your life, the one you have with yourself.

Yep! You heard me right. I did say YOU are most important.

Turn the page to find out why.

# PART ONE

# Relationships With Yourself

The most important relationship you're going to have in your life is the one you have with yourself. I mean getting to truly know and understand who you are, and how you tick. Identifying your wants and needs for yourself and your relationships. In order for you to feel comfortable in your own skin, you have to love your whole self: mind, body and spirit. In the following chapters we're going to dive in and learn all about how and why maintaining a good relationship within yourself is truly the best gift you can give to you and your relationships.

## BECASUE...

# Self Love!

Self-love. What is it, exactly? Well, it's something that we've most definitely been putting more emphasis on as a society over the last several years that's for sure! It's about the way we take care of ourselves on a whole. At least, that's how I define it with myself and my clients. It's about taking the time getting to know who you are in your most real and authentic way, and sharing your vulnerability with the world without hesitation. Self-love is about self-esteem, confidence, grace and about knowing your physical and emotional boundaries. Self-love is about imposing your own rules around the way you want to live your life. It's also making conscious and loving choices about who you want to spend your time with.

This idea of loving yourself isn't something that comes naturally for most of us. Well, we are born with all of the self-love we could need, but as we develop, and grow into society, many of us lose touch with that. Especially women. I tend to put everyone and everything else's needs before my own. All the time. Then when I do take some time for myself, I suffer from the guilt. Oy!

The guilt!! If you find yourself constantly putting other people's needs before your own, this proves that you've been well-trained to do the wrong thing for you. All of that guilt can mean that finding time for self-love — just for you — can take time to cultivate. In this section of the book, I'm going to share stories of my cultivation of self-love. Hopefully you see some of your own story in this.

## BECAUSE… *It's Your Most Important Relationship!*

For me, it took a while to develop a loving relationship with myself. It took me time to give that kind of attention to myself in a significant way. While I've always been a fan of "me time" in the way of manicures and things like that, it never occurred to me just how important it is to take time to refresh my energy.

It finally dawned on me when, a few years ago, one of my girl-friends suggested we go on a girl's trip — just us — for three days. No kids, no husbands. My son was 18 months old at the time and, because I needed it, I jumped at the chance. I had recently been through pregnancy, having a new baby, working full time, moving to a new neighborhood and a whole bunch of other things. I was feeling exhausted and needed to recharge.

My friend and I took a trip to the Dominican Republic. Three days of sun, sleep and spa time was exactly what we did. We weren't up late partying our faces off. We were doing the exact opposite! In fact, my girlfriend fell asleep one night with her book physically on her face. Lights were still on in the room. We were exhausted mothers. We needed to spend real time on ourselves so we could be fully present for our kids and our husbands when we got home.

That trip changed me. I became more aware of having the ability to choose time for myself without feeling guilty. I mean, it's totally okay for my child to spend time with my husband while I spent some time doing something for myself. It was hard to leave, but it ended up strengthening relationships all around.

21

I often need a bit of space from those I love to see myself clearly again. Even then it doesn't always happen overnight. That space is the self-love. It is the healthy boundary I need to feel like my whole self again. For a lot of us, it may take some major persuading, even in our own minds, to enforce that self-care, and take a moment away. I assure you, in the long run, it truly is life changing.

Your self-care doesn't need to be a fancy trip like we took. It could be taking a walk when you know you want one. Getting some space away from your children each week. Maybe for you it's a girl's night where you get to be you — without your normal responsibilities. Or a date night with your partner. Whatever it is that brings light, joy and spaciousness back to your world, please investigate it. Bring it in. Do it — on purpose. Know that it may feel uncomfortable at first. (Again, that's just that silly guilt). Do it anyway.

I know I said it already, but it bears repeating:

*The most important relationship you will ever have is the one you have with yourself.*

The ins and outs of self-love are not something I was taught as a child. People weren't talking about self-love like we are now at the time, back before the internet existed. I do think we've done a better job of it in recent years. I was taught about the importance of self-esteem and self- respect, but it wasn't explained in a way that was all encompassing, or practical. I didn't understand at the time how to do it. How do you do self-care on a daily basis?

What does it look like? It wasn't discussed in a way that made me think about myself holistically.

Let's talk about that idea for a moment. In my work, it means a few things when I refer to taking care of yourself holistically. It's about taking care of yourself physically, mentally and spiritually. It's about how we feel on each of these levels as we go through our day. It's about acknowledging those feelings and validating them. It's about embracing all of the parts of yourself and appreciating the things you can actually accomplish when you're in a fulfilling state. When you feel good, and full of self-love, you feel like you can do anything. You can take on the world.

Join me in a tiny experiment. Close your eyes and visualize what all-encompassing self-love means to you. What if someone loved you EXACTLY like you wanted and/or needed to be loved? What if someone loved you exactly as you are, unconditionally? What would that look like? Is it creating a routine that allows you to have some time for yourself on the daily? Is it surrounding yourself with the people you love because that energy fulfills you? There is no wrong answer — you know you the best. I just want you to understand that you're just as important as everyone else you're tending to — don't forget it! If you don't do this for you, who else could possibly know what you need?

When it came time for us to have our own children, my husband and I decided we would teach them about the importance of holistic self-love, like I am in this book. We try to be conscious about all of their choices from an early age — mind, body and spirit. Our holistic approach explains to them how to appreciate

23

the gifts they've been given. We introduced them to maintaining good physical health. We've also taught them tools to be able to deal with the ups and downs of life when they most certainly will arise. It is important in my family, especially since I'm a coach, that my children should start out with the idea that they love and appreciate themselves for who they are. We continue to build on that. Once they have a handle on respecting themselves, it makes it so much easier for them to respect others.

I know it can feel selfish (here's that guilt AGAIN) to dedicate time to yourself. It gets especially selfish feeling as we get older, and start families of our own. But seriously, please make time for yourself every day. No matter how chaotic your life is. Even if it's five minutes to have a quiet cup of coffee before all hell breaks loose in your house in the morning. You need that time. That time is actually making us better for our people. It allows us to be more present, less reactionary, or preoccupied. Believe me, I get it. One of my favorite things to say is, "Life gets in the way" and yet, that's never going to stop happening. It's up to you to ensure you make time for you.

## BECAUSE... *Your Needs Matter!*

I'm just going to say this out loud. Women tend to be martyrs. Carrying that martyr energy can make self-love feel almost painful — and selfish. I'm here to tell you that it only feels that way because you're not used to doing it. The same applies with your needs. Once you start communicating your needs, if you haven't been doing it for a while in relationships, it can give you that same guilt. But I'm here to start to put an end to the madness.

If you don't communicate your needs in a relationship, it means those needs aren't likely to get met. This sets the tone for the way you're going to create and sustain all of your other relationships. It's your job to make sure that your needs are met. No one else. If you take care of yourself and your needs with respect and love, others will follow suit.

Like I said, this stuff isn't always easy. In an effort to make my needs matter, I've had to go through some serious soul searching and self-introspection. I'm sure it started way earlier in life, but the fact that I wasn't taking care of my needs became very apparent for me several years ago, after I had Wyatt.

I was a new mom, not quite feeling like myself. I was uncertain about how I was going to navigate motherhood, a full-time job, and my husband all while looking at the world through very different glasses. I was feeling overwhelmed and I was trying to mask it in my busy-ness. I hope you can already see that I was definitely NOT taking care of my needs in this instance.

After some time of watching my frustration grow, my husband said to me, "Go spend some time on yourself." Wyatt was a few weeks old, my parents had left and we were alone with our little family, just the three of us. I was freaking out.

My next words fell out of my mouth in shock, "Whatever do you mean, spend some time on myself?"

"Go get your nails done, take a few hours and leave us here. We're fine."

"Of course you're fine, you're his father," I assured him. I'm not one for calling it babysitting when the dads are in charge. They're parents too. Give dads the respect they deserve.

"Well okay then. I'm going to get my nails done." That small gesture of him encouraging me to have some time to take care of my needs, no matter how small, was greatly appreciated!

How wonderful of this man who could see my need for self-care before I could. In fact, as I was walking to the nail salon I realized that I needed to spend more time learning all about this new version of me. By carrying, and then giving birth to my son, I felt like the new and enhanced Now-A-Mom version of myself. Was I a different person now that I had a child? What were my needs now from my husband? From myself? Were they different than before the baby? I now had an instant appreciation for every other mom in all of the Universe. I certainly felt different.

Being a mother did not mean I would have to lose myself — as so many other new mothers were proclaiming this at the time — and for some reason still are. The idea is a total crock of shit if you ask me. But, I'm going to save that soapbox opinion is for the *Why Am I Yelling? Because...Parenting* book!

Making my needs continue to matter, even though I had a new family, meant that while I loved and adored them, I had to continue to be myself. At the same time, I had to recognize, and still do, the things I wanted to focus on in my own life. For me, it meant that I needed to keep my life intact and add my family to it. I didn't want to stop reading the newspaper or learning about current events. I wanted to know more about them. I didn't want to stop socializing, and stay home with our new baby all the time. I wanted to bring him along and acclimate him to different places and surroundings. I didn't want to make it all about the baby either. I mean, one day my babies will leave home. I want my marriage to continue to live on strong! I wanted to continue to grow and improve. In order to do that, I needed to love me, and make my needs matter. It might be tough, but to me, ESSENTIAL.

Focus and intent were the first steps I took at becoming thoughtful of my needs on the regular. I asked myself all kinds of questions. What did I like about me? What didn't I like? What did I need more of in my life? What did I have too much of? I recognized that I needed better balance throughout my life. I was stretching myself too thin, trying to be everything for everyone. Ultimately, I was neglecting me. A sure-fire recipe for disaster.

I'm a big proponent of self-care for a few reasons, but mostly for what it does to my mind. It relaxes me. It makes me think about nothing and allows me to go into a place that I rarely get to visit because I'm constantly on the move or thinking about what's next in my day. Spending a chunk of time on yourself every so often (I would do it more regularly if my bank account allowed), is a great way to unwind and recharge.

Regardless of what you actually do, find a self-care routine that works for you and stick to it. It doesn't have to be elaborate. I know I need physical activity so a good walk or some time in the gym are my go to's. Focusing on how well you take care of yourself is a direct correlation to the way you view yourself. At the end of the day, it's nice to appreciate your self. The point is to do exactly that — take care of you.

## BECANSE... *You Need Your People!*

I started to get back into a routine after I had Wyatt. I stayed home with him for his first 10 months. My cousin lived in the same building as we did in Manhattan and she also had a new baby. We would take the boys on long walks through the city a few times a week to get some exercise for us and fresh air for them. It was a saving grace to have her so close by at the beginning of both of our journeys into motherhood. We could compare notes. There would be lots of, "Did you know this happens?" or, "I had no idea about that!" conversations between us. Mostly it was good to have someone who was in the same place I was at the same time. Someone to commiserate with me. It made life so much nicer.

After we moved to Brooklyn from downtown Manhattan, I was on my own. No bestie. New neighborhood, new baby. Just me and Wyatt out in the world while Will went to work. We would walk for hours, go to the park, then go home to make dinner. I tried to get outside as much as possible. I would let him nap in his stroller, and bring a book while we sat in the park. Reading was another thing I wanted to include in my daily routine. I wanted to devote more time to things I had started to neglect. Prior to having kids, I would read a book in a day or two. After them? Not so much. I was lucky to get in a book a month. It was killing me!

You know what else was killing me? And I was so painfully aware of it. I did not have enough time for socializing with other adults. I happen to be a very social person. I like talking and interacting with adult humans. I didn't particularly like being alone with a baby for hours on end. I missed having my cousin around so much! The other hard part was that there really weren't any other mom's in the park. It was mostly full of nannies or babysitters who hung out in their own groups. My poor husband, the minute he got home I would start talking his ear off! He probably wanted to wind down from his day, and there I was jabbering away. Surely that made him crazy, but because he's so amazing, he was almost always accommodating to my diatribes.

Feeling alone and isolated is not good for one's psyche, I will tell you that. I made the decision to go back to work when Wyatt was 10 months old because of it. Financially it was the right thing to do, yes. But even more so, I needed to be around my people — grownups. Having that tribe is clutch.

Socialization is definitely a self-love decision. I know a lot of people who would rather not be in a social setting — my husband included. I'm the exact opposite. I want people around all the time. I want our home to be filled with friends and family, kids running around, food being consumed, with laughter and a good time being had by all. Living in that small apartment in Brooklyn kept that to a minimum because I was so far away from everyone. Going back to work and having eight hours of adult interaction was just what I needed to feel like my brain was working. Baby Einstein is cute and all, but I needed the adult Einstein at that point, and I made that need matter.

## BECAUSE... *The Power of Purpose!*

My entire demeanor changed when I went back to work. I felt like I had a purpose for myself as a stand-alone human. Obviously being a mother was important, but I also remembered that I did not exist just for my child. Did I have guilt? To be honest, I didn't. We had hired a wonderful nanny to take care of Wyatt. I felt like she was completely capable and engaging with him in the same ways I would have been.

On my first day back at work, I came home and our nanny looked at me and said "I can't believe you didn't check in once. That's never happened to me." With that simple statement, I felt all of the guilt tsunami hit me. I felt like I had done something wrong! Not checking in on my baby? What kind of mother was I? I explained to her, but more for myself, that I felt confident in what was happening at home, and if there was something I needed to be made aware of, I was sure she would call me. I asked her if she was offended. She smiled and said, "No way, it's awesome that you're so comfortable with having me here." That immediately made me feel better. I let go of a tiny bit of my self judgement.

I've said this before, but community is so important. Being around adults was exactly what I needed to feel better about myself too. I got to put on nice clothes and wear my high heels again. I wore makeup and had intelligent conversations. I went out to lunch and sometimes even drank wine! On occasion I would go out after work to an adult function, or with the girls for dinner and cocktails. I was slowly regaining some of my former life back that I hadn't realized I had missed. I was redefining my purpose in the world, and It was making a big difference in my attitude and the way I felt about myself.

Creating a comfortable place for ourselves, surrounded by the ones we love, is crucial when you're building a life for yourself and your family. But it shouldn't cause you to lose sight of your purpose. And quite honestly, that purpose can change. At one time my purpose was to find my new self after having a baby. These days my purpose it's focusing on creating a legacy for them. Really knowing the person you are, and living through your purpose with confidence is truly inspiring.

*You see? It's not selfish to love yourself and make yourself a priority. It's the exact opposite! When you allow yourself the space you deserve your confidence boosts. Your outlook changes and your appreciation of yourself becomes a strength. Give yourself the time you need to focus on becoming the person you are continually growing into. Start by loving yourself.*

*Now it's time to love our bodies...*

## BECAUSE...

# Body Love!

When you think about body love what's the first thing that comes to mind? If you're asking me that question my answer is physical appearance. But honestly, it's way more than that. While physical appearance is something we should be aware of, it's not the end all be all of body love. Body love is about loving who you are from a physical perspective. Everything from the way you take care of yourself through nutrition and exercise to the way you present yourself. It's about self-esteem and how to rise up from self-imposed limitations.

It's really important to understand the pieces that go into loving your body on a whole. In this section I'm talking about learning how to overcome body image and self-esteem issues, paying attention to the way you take care of yourself and finding a comfortability with who you are. That is what body love is all about.

## BECAUSE... *Love That Bod, It's Your Only One!*

Oh how I wish we could all just love how we look and feel when it comes our own bodies. I feel like I have spent an inordinate amount of time trying to fix my "flaws." Flaws that only exist in my mind. If you've been following along, you already know that's not how we should be doing it. Body love is about taking the best care of your physical vehicle as you can. For me, it's making good choices when it comes to nutrition and health. I tell my kids all the time, your body is the one thing you have a lot of control over. From the food you put into it, to the activity you do with it, to the maintenance you use to care for it. Your body should be treated intentionally, and with kindness and respect so that it can last for a long time.

I believe in whole self-care. Taking care of my body is just as important as taking care of my mind and spirit. Because of my family history, I'm a big believer in moderation. I mean, life's short. We should experience it fully, while exercising good judgement *most* of the time. No one is asking you to be perfect. Just remember that you only have one body. Make it last!

I grew up in a home where food was pretty much the center of the universe with my parents. To this day while we sit at the breakfast table and start our morning together, the first question that floats from my mother's mouth is, "What do you want to have for lunch and dinner?" Every. Single. Time. Um, hello? I'm still chewing my BREAKFAST! I'm not thinking about what I'm going to eat until I get hungry again.

My dad had a heart attack in 2002 that resulted in him having a triple bypass. He came home from the hospital with a new lifestyle plan: things he could and could not eat, way less sodium intake, exercise more regularly, stop smoking. It was a full recipe for turning his physical health around. Unfortunately, that new lifestyle didn't last very long. He went back to his old ways of eating. That continued for another fifteen years, and as a result, his health paid for it over and over again. He suffered a stroke and additional heart episodes that required multiple small procedures every few years. Each of his health failures compounded into a domino effect that caused severe kidney damage. He would eventually have to have dialysis three times a week for two years until his body couldn't sustain any more. His ultimate sacrifice was his life, at the far-too-young age of seventy-one.

I often wonder about the choices he made when it came to his health. If he had stuck to the regimen sent home with him all those years ago, how different would his path have been? Would he not have experienced several setbacks throughout those last years? I wonder if he would still be alive now if he made his body health a priority. Unfortunately, I can't change things for him. But, I take those painful lessons for myself, and to show others how to do it differently.

My mom's health is not much different from my father's. She's been diabetic for as long as I can remember, requiring medication to maintain her health. She's also had heart issues, albeit genetic (my grandmother had the same ailment) requiring her to have valve replacement surgery a few years ago. It truly is amazing to me that the possibility that some, (maybe not all) of my parent's health issues could've been addressed by exercise and diet. Yet, they never made a commitment to fix it. Why? It's something I struggle with as an adult and a parent. For me it would be an easy decision: make the necessary changes to have the life I want to live, and to be active as I continue to age.

As their daughter, it's been frustrating to witness my parents make the choices they did with their health and bodies. It's been an ongoing conversation for too many years to count. My mother complains about her weight, talks about the latest diet she's going to attempt, which ultimately lasts for all of a hot second, then starts the cycle all over again. We've since stopped talking about it. My mom knows how I feel. She knows that I understand that willpower is not easy for her.

I have learned to look at my body differently. I have developed my willpower over time. I can turn it on when I need to so that I don't have too much. It's so much more fun this way. I can enjoy all the foods without all of those shitty guilt feelings.

I'm going to say this again. You only get one body. There may be a technology way in the future that changes that, but for the moment, it's true. Do you want to be here for as long as possible for your family? To keep the adventure going? Then take care of the vehicle that takes you everywhere. That doesn't mean restriction. It just means balance. That's not so bad.

## BECAUSE... *Food Rules!*

I mean...I love ALL THE FOOD!!! Making healthy choices when it comes to fueling my body, especially because I have kids, is something I take seriously. We try to teach them the importance of the different types of foods we eat. We try to eat as organically as possible, but we're realistic about it. Being realistic with eating creates balance. Being unrealistic, well, it creates problems in another way. Let me share a story about my husband.

Will grew up in a household that didn't really have any kind of junk food. As a result, he's become a big snack food junkie as an adult. He told our little guy, Elias, that when he was younger, his parents used to scrape the cream from the middle of the Vienna Fingers sandwich cookies before they ate them. They did this because his parents felt the cookies had too much sugar. Elias, my youngest, was dumbfounded because all he eats is the cream and leaves the cookie. Because of the unrealistic view of having very limited amounts of junk food growing up, my husband will try any kind of chip or candy bar! His candy willpower is way out of balance.

See! Restrictions and being unrealistic with yourself and your family create their own set of problems. I try to have a healthy compromise in our home. But we don't forbid sweets either. We have chosen to demonstrate balance around food choices.

Another way this balance shows up is in the way we deal with trying new foods. Dun, dun, duuuun. Yes, we are believers in trying new things. I know that food is a major control issue for most kids. So in our house, we have a rule when it comes to trying foods. The Three Strike Rule. You have to try something three times before you decide you don't like it. It seems to have worked with some things (broccoli for my big kid) and not with others (brussels sprouts with my little guy). Yes, I have cookies and chips in the closet, but I also have tons of fruit, yogurt and healthy choices on hand as an alternative. Balance.

My personal relationship with food has always been pretty good. I've gotten better as I've aged. I've become more aware of the importance of label reading, and knowing where our food comes from. Knowing what you put in your body is most certainly a way of loving your body.

Another way to love what I put into my body, is to cook. Even if it's just for myself. I started cooking at a very young age. This was inspired by my Grandma Jean. She and I would spend hours in the kitchen talking and cooking. She was always talking about the importance of fresh ingredients, and how she rarely used things with preservatives in them. She cooked with a lot of love. I remember learning how to make things like chicken cutlets, fresh broccoli with garlic and oil, meatballs and all kinds of pasta dishes. There was even a time when my parents made our pasta. It was short lived because it can be a pain in the ass, but it did happen.

Cooking is one of my favorite things to do. I love it. I especially love to try new things. I don't have many aversions. But, there is one thing that grosses me out. The one thing I will not eat is bananas. I think it's a texture and smell thing. I just cannot stomach them, and I've tried more than three times! Beyond bananas, I'll pretty much try anything at least once. The food I prepare at home is pretty normal stuff. My boys aren't particularly picky eaters, but they're not the most adventurous either. What's important for me is that they're getting a well-balanced diet. I try to feed their growing brains and bodies with stuff that keeps them healthy.

I'm also a big fan of going out or ordering in from restaurants, because... balance. Especially since I live in one of the greatest food cities in the world. New York City has some of the most amazing restaurants. How could we resist? What's even better is that in many cases you can probably have some of the best food of your life on the cheap. Food trucks, dollar dumplings, Mexican food and even greasy pizza — all at your fingertips. Multiple course tasting menus, fancy sushi, STEAKHOUSES. I could go on and on and on... I love it all! BUT I know I can't do it every night. Like I said in the beginning of this chapter, I don't believe in depravation, I believe in balance!

# BECAUSE... *Everything In Moderation!*

There are two ways that I know of to deal with moderation. Either having a cheat day that you get to eat whatever and how much of it you want. Or, choose to try whatever you want, and don't eat the whole thing. Either works as a way to allow yourself some guilty pleasures without going crazy. I know I can't have some things on a regular basis, but if I eat with the understanding that it's not necessarily the best option, I can still enjoy it every once in a while. Hello ice cream. Come to mama!

The most important thing I try to impress upon my family when it comes to fueling our bodies is moderation. It's okay to allow yourself to indulge, but make sure you're making up for it by being conscious with the healthy choices. Do not skip meals. (My husband is the worst at this). Eat the good stuff on the regular, because if you don't you're not getting rewarded with any of the bad stuff for dessert.

Of course, when you have kids they don't understand moderation. They understand the opposite — inhaling food. It's our job to teach them. My kids could literally stand in front of the snack cabinet and eat one of everything in a sitting. No. They are not hungry. They just know it's there, so they eat it.

Having two growing boys and a husband with a growing boy appetite, we go through a lot of food in our house. My boys are still young. I'm not sure what's gonna happen when they're both teenagers! (God help me, and our pantry!)

Just the other night, my husband was trying to explain to our little one the difference between hunger and availability. The conversation went something like this:

"Mom, I'm hungry."

"No you're not, Elias, we just finished dinner."

"But I didn't have bessert yet." (That's how he pronounces dessert. He's 5. I will savor it for as long as I can!)

"Ok, well, you can have bessert in a few minutes. Rest your belly and play with your toys for a bit."

3 minute lapse…"Mom, I'm getting bessert."

"Ok, get bessert."

He then comes back with a 2-pack of chocolate chip cookies. Fine. He promptly inhales said cookies.

5 minute lapse…

"Mom, I'm hungry."

To which I reply, "You have no idea what hunger is!" I say as my frustration meter increases.

At this point, my husband chimes in and says, "There is no way you're hungry. You need to learn the difference between hunger and availability." He goes on to try to explain to our five year-old that he can't eat everything in sight just because it's there to eat. We go through this ritual every single night. Sometimes I give in and allow him to have yogurt before bed. In my head it's like when they were infants — send them to bed with a full belly and they'll sleep better. I'm not sure if this theory works but if we get to go to bed happy without a tantrum, then I'm all for it! Because...balance.

## BECAUSE... *For Those Who Enjoy A Cocktail!*

I love a cocktail. That's for sure. But at the same time drinking, or over drinking, is something that runs in both mine and my husband's families. When I was much younger I could knock them back with the best of them. I mean, you're looking at the girl who found out she was pregnant with her first child the day after St. Patrick's Day. If you're not familiar with St. Patrick's Day in New York City, it's basically a national holiday that begins by waking up with a beer and ends by going to bed with a beer. I believe I was doing shots and dancing on a bar at one point that evening. Clearly, I've had my share of over indulging when it comes to cocktailing. But once the kids showed up, drinking as a sport faded out of my life. I just had too much to do!

I like to have my wits about me and remember the conversations I've had the night before. It doesn't feel good to be hungover. It's exhausting — especially with kids around. Kids can suck the fun out of partying bigtime. I can appreciate a good glass of wine or a fun cocktail these days and be good with one or two. The idea of waking up the next day feeling clear-headed is way more enticing than the alternative. Regardless of what you choose for yourself, choose it consciously. Have another glass of wine, but be considerate of your body in the process.

Basically what I'm saying is, be aware of how you're treating yourself from the inside. The way you feel has a direct correlation with way more than you think. It goes deeper than merely functioning. The way you feel attributes to your attitude, your appearance and your overall health. Make good choices when it comes to what you put in your body. You wouldn't put crappy gas in a Maserati would you? Treat yourself like you're a Maserati and give yourself the best gift of health you can. You deserve to feel good. Don't you?

## BECAUSE... *Move Your Booty!*

Body health, for me, also includes exercising. You know, that thing that makes you sweat and swear at the same time? As a person who wasn't really taught the value of exercise, I had to learn it on my own. I've got to tell you, I'm hardly athletic. At. All. I was a ballet dancer as a kid. I took some tennis lessons for a hot minute. That was about it. Unless of course, you count the hours I spent sweating on the dance floor at various night clubs throughout college and my twenties. In that case, I would be the queen of exercising! But seriously, I didn't know the value of it and couldn't find the fun in it when I was a lazy sloth kid. So shameful!

It wasn't until I was in my twenties that I decided to join a gym. Throughout the last two decades I've dabbled in kickboxing (so fun!), had an addiction to spin classes (best ass I've ever had), and I worked with personal trainers (after giving birth). After all of this effort, I've realized that I have become someone who needs to have some kind of physical movement in my life with regularity. I've learned that for me, it's more fun to mix it up rather than do the same thing every day.

I also realized that I don't need to go to a gym every time to actually exercise. I'm a busy mom with two kids, a husband and a business. I fit my movement in whenever I can. I do yoga on my kitchen floor thanks to some great apps that I've downloaded. I paddleboard in the summer on the lake. I do squats while I dry my hair. You should see me. It's quite a hilarious sight and causes fits of giggles from the small child. I also walk — a lot — especially living in New York City. Our feet are our main mode of transportation. I do hit the gym when the mood strikes, but in all seriousness, if I can find 30 - 45 minutes a day to break a sweat, get my blood pumping and move around, that counts as exercise. While I know the idea of consistent exercising doesn't necessarily appeal to many, when you break it down the way I do, it really doesn't feel like a chore. I'm basically incorporating exercise into what works in my life. I walk Elias to school (almost) every day. That's about two miles round trip. That is a good little walk in the morning. And it totally counts as exercise. Check!

Of course, having two active boys is helpful on the movement front. Running around after them for the last twelve years has kept all of us on our toes. Even though both boys are very physically active with extracurricular sports, we try to keep it going when they're not in an organized setting. Going to the park, playing outside with friends and kicking around a soccer ball on a Saturday afternoon is good for them. And me.

## BECABSE... *You Are Beautiful!*

Eating right and exercise are super important when maintaining body health, but my definition of beauty is loving how you look. Now, I fully recognize not everyone is model gorgeous. My gray hairs are coming in faster than I would prefer. That's not what I'm talking about when I talk about being beautiful.

What really makes people beautiful comes from the inside. Not the outside. I'm talking about confidence, self-esteem and ability to fully love yourself and others. In order to fully love yourself you have to love the body you were given — exactly the way you were created — imperfections and all. I tell my kids all the time, we are all equally beautiful regardless of how their opinion of what's happening on the outside. Everyone deserves to be treated with kindness and respect. We are all beautiful — just the way we are.

Being comfortable in our own skin isn't easy for everyone. It certainly wasn't for me. You'll hear more about that later. Sometimes loving your body takes conscious effort. Especially in our superficial society where we are led to believe that there is only one standard of beauty. Most people have many things they don't like about their own body. Those people who glow are the ones who own and love every ounce who they are inside out.

Going through all the phases and stages of maturity, from being an awkward and confused teenager to blossoming into a full-blown adult, can make it feel hard to love that body that just won't quit changing. Neither you, nor I, can expect to come out of it unscathed. Those beauty expectations can be damaging if you are someone who takes that stuff to heart.

If you feel sensitive to the opinions of others, just know that there are a lot of us out there. I can remember being a teenager and wanting all the latest fashion and makeup because *Cosmo* said it was cool. My mom wasn't as into it. I can remember kids being made fun of because they didn't have the latest name brand slapped on their asses. Insecurity about how we look to others is a real thing. I was recently on a class trip with Wyatt to the Museum of Natural History. We took a bunch of public school seventh graders to see the dinosaurs. There were other schools from all over NYC there that day, including some private schools. All of a sudden, the girls huddled up, and were visibly affected. I could see that something was going on — so I headed over to find out what was going on.

What was shocking, was what I actually heard them say as I walked up. "Oh, they must have a lot of money." "I wish I could go to private school." "They must be better off than we are." "Oh, I bet they don't live in Brooklyn." I was floored. These girls had made some grand assumptions, about this other class of kids, and themselves, based on the fact that these kids had on burgundy, private-school blazers. They had immediately assumed that these kids had more money, and they had less.

I saw this as a perfect opportunity for teaching moment! Being a former uniform wearing private school kid, I quickly turned the scenario around. "You guys, those uniforms do not dictate the economic status of the kids! While yes, there are some parents who could afford the tuition to private school, it typically doesn't come without sacrifice." I also told them that some of the students could be on scholarship, and still another reason kid's go to private school is because the public schools in their neighborhoods are not as good as ours. I also told them that when I was a kid in private school, I wished I could wear whatever I wanted the way they did. I told the girls I bet the private school kids would love to be wearing their street clothes to school. I finished my teaching moment by telling them that in the end, it doesn't matter what you wear, it matters the kind of person you are. The girl's perspective changed in two minutes. There are two sides to every coin, right?

The important thing to remember is that you are more than the opinions of the people around you. You are even more than your opinion of yourself! You're an amazing and beautiful being with value simply because you are here, and alive. You are extension of Source/God/Universe/Oneness. No one can change that. That fact cannot be changed by you, and it most certainly cannot be changed by an opinion from someone else. So deal with it — you ARE beautiful.

When we're in the moment of being criticized for our looks by our self, or someone else, it can feel easy to think the material stuff is important — especially when we're younger. "If I just had that new dress, I'd be pretty." "Or I had those shoes, people would finally see that I'm amazing." The reality is that as you get older you come to understand that none of that really matters. The people who mean something to you have that meaning because they have been loving. They have been supportive. They were there when you needed them. And vice versa. They understand and appreciate your boundaries. Remember the 5 Essentials?

If you are feeling a lack of love for your body, it's time to start appreciating what really matters about you. Those inside parts.

It's time to decide that you love you no matter what. Own your look. Embrace it. Even the things about you that feel difficult to love. Love those things the most! Find comfort in what you love about you, and shout that out to the world. Remember that you are beautiful — just because you breathe.

## BECAUSE... *Your Scars Don't Define You!*

Your self-confidence is something that needs tending to — all the time. Otherwise, it can waver. There will always be someone smarter, prettier, more successful, than you (blah, blah, blah). Instead of being self-conscious and/or critical of each other, how about you focus on being comfortable in your own skin? It's no use to be constantly comparing yourself to others. Fall in love with the gifts you were given, and celebrate them. Self-confidence is sexy!

I guarantee the way you see yourself is not how others see you. Especially if you focus on your "flaws." I've been known to point out a jiggle or a roll on my body on occasion to my husband. He lovingly says to me, "I have no idea what you're talking about." Clearly, he's a smart guy. He won't even engage in the body conversation with me for even a moment. You get what I'm saying. The things we often obsess over are things most people don't notice.

You might look in the mirror and see all the "wrong" things, yet those tend to be the exact things our partners are the most attracted to. I know my husband does not care that my stomach isn't as firm or flat as it used to be. This stomach carried his two children. He loves it more now. Right, honey? (wink, wink). He doesn't care that my hair has been going gray since my mid-twenties. In fact, he thinks I should grow it out and see how it looks. That's because we used to live in the same building as a famous model with gray hair. We've both been obsessed with the fact that she could embrace her natural beauty — gray hair and all. But again, she's a model and well, I'm not. I'm definitely not ready for that. Aaah! I just did it to myself! That is EXACTLY what I'm talking about.

For all the criticisms I have of myself, maybe I should take a good hard look in the mirror, and look at each criticism as a life lesson instead. Each mark on my body tells a story — sometimes good — and sometimes not so good. They are representations of times in my life that can remind me of who I am, and sometimes, where I came from. It's almost like reading the pages of a book. Finding the way to love myself no matter what is the key.

My son loves to hear the story about the scar on his chin. When Wyatt was two years old, he was running around my best friend's house in Florida while we were visiting over the holidays. He tripped and fell and sliced his chin wide open. Thank goodness my friend was a nurse and had contacts at the local hospital. My poor little guy needed seven stitches after an hour of the attending trying without success to glue his chin together. The doctor was so patient. He was being as gentle as he could be with my toddler. When he realized he wasn't going to be able to close the cut without stitches, he explained to us that he needed Wyatt to be restrained. They actually put my sweet boy in a straight-jacket to administer the stitches.

Watching the doctor put a six-inch needle into my child's face almost made me pass out. I can remember my friend reminding me to breathe. It was awful not being able to help in any way other than to try to comfort my baby. It was so hard to watch. It was over in a few short minutes, yet it felt like hours. We were all so relieved and exhausted when it was over. Poor Wyatt was so good and tried so hard not to freak out. What an awful experience for a little kid.

He is now as a tween, and has absolutely no recollection of it. Will and I, on the other hand, are scarred for life. I'm pretty sure I cried for a long time after he was asleep that night. Now he's fine and that's all that matters! As he's gotten older, he sometimes looks at it and makes a remark about its visibility. (There is literally none as it's under his chin, but he sees it.) So, I tell him it's all part of his story. And we should love every part of our story, even the bumps, scrapes and scars because they're what make us who we are.

*Your body is a temple. I'm sure you've heard that a time or two, right? It really is true. It's easy to take care of the beauty on the outside. But it goes beyond that. Remember that you are responsible for maintaining our beauty on the inside too. Creating good habits, using moderation and treating yourself like the bright, shiny temple you are is crucial for your health. Make sure you're taking care of you the best way you can.*

## BECAUSE...

## Mind Love!

The mind is a beautiful and complex thing. It is an incredible tool if you use it that way. It can really help you create an amazing, fulfilling life, or if neglected, your mind can absolutely sabotage your progress. If you keep your mind healthy, by feeding it with positivity, unconditional love and knowledge, your mind will work in support of you and your life. On the other hand, it's easy for the mind to get caught in a trap of self-destruction. I mean, we've all been there. Getting stuck in your head, about anything, can take you on a real downward spiral of self-doubt.

When you work on taking care of your mind, you'll have the ability to change that mindset with the flip of a switch. Powerful stuff happens when you put your mind to work. Life changes, abundance enters, horizons expand, opportunities abound. It truly is an amazing thing.

## BECAUSE... *The Power of Positivity!*

Oh, our minds are powerful, tricky things, aren't they? Human beings are so quick to think negative thoughts about themselves and their surroundings that it can be difficult to dig ourselves out of the hole. I'm not sure how this practice of self-deprecation and negativity became something we do to ourselves, but I know it's not helpful.

I am a believer in the power of positivity. I believe in having a mindset practice that helps you focus on creating an optimistic attitude. This means using affirmations and the power of my mind to create or shift a mood, belief or feeling based on what my needs are in the moment. Like for example, when I'm about to speak at an event and I need to calm my nerves. I use positive affirmations to calm down, focus and be present in the moment.

I also believe I have an obligation to teach this ability to my children from the day they are born. Giving our children the power to soothe themselves and choose their feelings allows them to learn and understand how important their power truly is. It can be something as simple as teaching them positive affirmations for when they're feeling anxious or stressed.

I can remember one night when Wyatt was acting off. Something wasn't right. I couldn't put my finger on it. When I asked him about it, he insisted everything was fine. It wasn't until he went to bed that I heard him crying into his pillow. It took a few minutes to get him to calm down. Once I finally did, I asked him what was wrong. He said he failed a pop quiz in math, and he didn't want me to be disappointed because of it. After I breathed a sigh of relief that it wasn't something earth shattering, I explained to him that he would probably fail more tests in his life, given how many were to come in the future, and that it was going to take a lot more than that to disappoint me. He started to relax.

We then started talking about how stressful school can be. I shared with him that when I feel stressed, I use mantras and positive affirmations to help me through the emotional wave of it. I told him to "let it go" and to repeat those words over a few times while taking deep breaths to try to calm his nerves. I also assured him that there was nothing he couldn't come to me (or his dad) with that would make us judge him without a fair discussion. He recited the mantra with me and used the deep breathing. He was off to dreamland in no time. The power of positivity works!

Having a positive view of yourself and who you are as a person isn't just about being physically healthy. It includes your mental and spiritual health as well. Being in sync with all the components of your makeup is the first step to maintaining any successful relationship in your life.

Your mindset affects your life more than most people realize. And usually, those mindset patterns start young. If you're raised in an encouraging, motivating and positive environment, it is a lot easier for you to put that same energy out into the universe. If you were raised in a negative environment you have a choice to make: continue the negativity, or find the positivity. I'm lucky that my background is from the positive. My parents were very encouraging of us kids growing up which is why we place a big emphasis on creating a positive environment in our home.

## BECAUSE... *You Have To Practice!*

My mindset practice is so important, I do it daily. There are magical practices I do for myself throughout the day when I need it. My mindset practice makes me more powerful. It helps me work through a problem, or reach a goal feeling positive and empowered no matter the difficulty.

Mindset practices are fairly new for me, within the last couple of years. When I started my own business, I noticed my stress level and intolerance for things were becoming elevated. I was starting to react to everything. I spoke to a mindset coach. She helped me realize that I had the power to control my thoughts in a more positive way. I just had to become more aware of them.

She suggested I start writing in a journal. I loved that idea because it wasn't something I was unfamiliar with. I kept a journal for years in college, and for a while afterward. Journaling now has allowed me to get my thoughts out of my mind and body, where they will do no good, and put them onto paper where I can more easily observe them. No matter how big or small the thought is, writing it out has helped me work through things with more clarity. It is difficult to change things you are unaware of. Journaling has given me more awareness around my thoughts, and has helped me to learn how to visualize situations and their solutions more clearly.

I also started to speak my intentions and affirmations — out loud. I have a few mantras that I live by. Some mantras I've been using for many years. It never occurred to me to speak them out, or to write them down. Once I started to say them out loud, I noticed a change in my outlook. I felt stronger and more empowered. I started taking braver actions.

Choosing a mantra or affirmation doesn't have to be difficult. One of mine is "Deep faith eliminates fear." It was actually the quote I used in my high school yearbook. That's how long I've been saying it! If I'm feeling uneasy or nervous about something, I find myself repeating that mantra over, and over in my head. It might take a few tries to find one or two that feel good to you, but once you do I highly recommend using them. Shoot for any mantra that makes you feel better, and more empowered than your current circumstance. It's really been helpful for me! Especially in the hours between dinnertime and bedtime. I typically repeat one about patience during those hours. You know what I'm sayin' parents?

I begin and end every day by giving thanks and repeating mantras. Before I get out of bed, I lay there and say a little prayer of give thanks for another day that I get to be alive. It's that simple. I say thank you for the day that lays ahead of me, whatever that may be, and I give it up to God.

I get up and take care of my kids, school routine, ya know...but after that I get to spend some time on myself. I do a journal entry and write my affirmations down five times each, all while repeating them over in my head. Then I do a little meditation on my yoga mat in my kitchen (that's where the sunshine is in the mornings) for about 10 minutes. I make my tea and start my day. If I'm having any feelings of stress or anxiety, I refer back to one of my affirmations to help me through it. At bedtime I do some deep breathing exercises and another round of giving thanks. Taking stock in my day and giving thanks for my experiences helps me realize everything I accomplished.

Even though I do all of the mindset work available, not every day is champagne and roses! The title of this section is for real. It is a practice. Some days there might be something weighing heavy on my mind. but instead of the worry, I try to give thanks — even for the tough days. By giving thanks for even the tough days, I'm acknowledging that strife exists, and that I am going to work on it. I find that doing these things before closing my eyes allows me to have a better night's sleep — until the small child comes in and wakes me up because he needs to snuggle. Yes, that happens on occasion.

## BECAUSE... *Mindset Can Be A Struggle!*

Self-esteem issues were not uncommon for me, especially when I was a teenager. I mean, I've basically had the same body I currently have since I was 13 years old. Curves, boobs and all. Couple that with pubescent acne and you have a recipe for some serious insecurities. Especially since we moved during some of the most delicate years of my teen life, I felt uneasy and inadequate. I wondered if the kids at my new school would like the new kid from New York? Would they accept me? Would they make fun of me? I did finally find my footing, and boys came into the picture. It then became about whether I thought they would find me pretty enough.

Now I know what you're saying to yourself. "You should never think that about yourself, Krista." But in the 80's, there wasn't an empowerment movement for girls. We weren't taught that we could do anything the boys could do — at least I don't remember that. It was all about how we looked, and what we wore. Peers judged you for your size and appearance. We judged ourselves to make sure we fit in. Being a teenager sucked, and I didn't have it that bad!

I think we do a much better job as parents these days to make sure our kids are all encompassing when it comes to communication, self-esteem and identity issues. With so much information at our disposal, it's easy to know what's happening in your children's lives if you're vigilant. It's my job to be an observer. I check my son's text messages and emails. He's 12, that's my job. I want to make sure he's okay.

Mindset issues can creep in teenagers and become and epidemic quickly. Even though I'm pretty sure he's very sweet and kind,

I want him to know he's being watched so that as he gets older he can then make the right choices for himself in regard to how to treat others. He will have the understanding that the mind is a fragile instrument, and that words, if not used properly, can be hurtful and demeaning. My son is very observant. He sees the news and social media. He knows what's going on, and if he doesn't he isn't afraid to ask. We try, as parents to be on top of delicate subjects but not too in his face for fear of the communication shut down. If I lay in too heavy with the fear, at some point he'll stop listening. It's a slippery slope with tweenagers.

That's why I believe mindset work should be introduced at an early age. I have the tools to show them encouragement, support and love. Those tools will assist them in understanding that having the right mindset can alter any situation in their favor. Having a positive mindset takes practice though — that's for sure! That's why I'm there. To help with the practice. I have to be in a place of truth and honesty to do so. That's why it's easier to start with the little ones, because their innocence is a good thing. They haven't been tainted with too many negative influences that they don't understand yet!

I like to do mindset practice with my kids at bedtime. We have a routine that consists of us all getting into bed and talking about our day. Then we take turns and tell a story about one good thing that happened and why we're grateful for it. It makes us all feel good and allows the boys to fall asleep with a positive thought in their heads. So simple, right? We sometimes do deep breathing exercises if one of them is feeling anxious about a big day at school or a game coming up. My kids go to bed every night with an I love you and some encouragement.

# BECAUSE... *Get Your Heart & Mind In Alignment!*

As we get older our mindset work takes on a whole new meaning. It can pull us out of ruts and change the course of our lives. I am a testament to that, I believe it completely. I was in a not-so-great place a few years ago, struggling with having to make a decision professionally and not really knowing what to do. I felt like I would be failing my family if I turned my back on my high paying, stable job yet I felt like I would be failing myself if I stayed. My heart and head were speaking two different languages.

My decision revealed itself in the form of a co-worker, someone in a position higher than mine starting to say inappropriate things to me and others in our workplace. I would often tell him he couldn't say the things he was saying about his direct reports and try to calmly guide him along the right path. Not having it. I believe he has what a lot of people refer to as a "Napoleon Complex," and he displayed narcissistic and sociopathic behavior. On a few occasions he said things to me about my appearance that made me feel uncomfortable and quite frankly infuriated. Upon going to his direct report, and to the Human Resources department in the company, and having nothing done about my inquiry, I realized that my mind was made up. I could not stay in that space. Here's the thing you guys, my self-respect has always been intact. I know that I will survive. In fact, I know that I will do better than merely survive. I was not going to allow myself to be the victim. I was not going to drag on in an unhealthy environment either. I made the decision to leave the company. I have not for one minute regretted that decision.

Even though I knew what I had to do, the struggle was real. The paycheck was good, the schedule was good, the flexibility was good. The treatment was bad. I'm sure I could've stayed and moved to a different spot within the company, however, my long tenure there and the direction the company was taking forced me to take a look at my life with a raw understanding of the good and the bad. It was hard to do. I had to peel back all of the layers of the onion and check the core. My core. It was time to move on.

In order to make the most powerful decision here, I had to make sure my head was in the right place to match my heart. I had to spent some time really thinking about what was important to me in my heart, and what was important to the professional future I wanted to have. Thankfully, I've always had the support of my husband who is an excellent sounding board and my voice of reason. I took a moment to get in alignment before I made my decision, so I knew what I needed to do. It's the best decision I ever made.

Upon leaving the company I had been a part of for 16 years, I felt a million pounds lighter. I had no idea what I wanted to be when I grew up but I knew I didn't want to be where I was. That's when my soul-searching journey truly began. I spent my days trying to figure out how to find a job, except I didn't want a "job." I wanted a future. I wanted something bigger. I turned to a career placement services company and ended up working with a career coach. She helped me change my life. I took tons of self-assessments, quizzes and learned all about the art of marketing yourself. I updated my LinkedIn profile, and started creating new resumes and cover letters. It was only after I did all of that work, that I realized something very important. For all of the interviews I was going on, none of them were exciting me.

I was on the phone with my coach one afternoon. We were having a heart-to-heart. She suggested to me that I explore coaching for myself as a profession. I balked at first, because I mean, what does a coach do in real life? She cracked up. She told me there are all different kinds of coaches, and walked me through how she became one. I was intrigued. In a matter of days I had researched several certification courses, and had conducted a few interviews for the courses I was interested in. I was so excited, and nervous, internally questioning my decisions, wondering about the outcome, trying to envision the future. But mostly excited that I knew deep down that this was the right path for me. Again, I found alignment between my mind and my heart. A new path opened!

Luckily for me, my husband knew too. I can remember sitting in our kitchen, waiting for a call from a prospective employer. It was the final call with their Human Resources folks, and I knew I did not want the job. When my husband found me sitting alone, he asked me what was going on. I told him I didn't want that job, that I wanted to finish my certification and try my hand at coaching. He looked me right in the eye and said, well then, that's what you have to do. You can't not do this. Take a leap, go for it. So I did.

My mindset at the time was clear and certain. I would sit and meditate and pray about what the right thing to do was. I would ask the universe, my guardian angel, and God (covering all my bases) at the same time to guide me. I was always pointed in the more difficult direction, but it was always the right one and I knew it in my heart. Have you felt that kind of alignment about anything? Getting clear on what your mind and heart wants may take some time. Make sure you are doing the introspection work, and keeping your mind empty of chatter. By focusing on the big picture, you will prevail.

*Here's the thing, I'm convinced that when you invest the time in focusing on your mindset, all kinds of wonderful shifts will happen. Introducing the practice of using positive affirmations and mantras can change your attitude in a split second. When you have a firm grip on your mind love, you will attract goodness and positivity into your life, and you will see clearly the path that you are creating for yourself.*

## BECAUSE...

# Spiritual Love!!

Now that we've got our bodies and minds covered, let's move on to spirit. Spiritual love is something that's taken work for me as I've grown as a person and become a mother. I haven't always felt in line with church going. As a young person, I didn't understand the difference between religion, and spirituality. Now as an adult, I do. For me, having a spiritual connection to something greater than yourself is important. It makes me feel supported, watched over and connected to a larger energy that brings me comfort especially in times of reflection and intro-spection. Religion and spirituality are based on personal belief, and I happen to believe in all of it — God, the Universe, Angels, Spirit. Any help I can get is welcome into my life!

## BECAUSE... *Going to Church Doesn't Mean You're Connected!*

I was raised Catholic, I even went to Catholic grade school. Every Sunday I would attend church with my family. I memorized all the prayers, and participated in the ceremony of sit, stand, kneel, but the thing is, I don't remember ever getting anything out of going to church, other than socializing in the parking lot when mass was over. When I was a kid I did not equate church with spirituality. For me it meant asking for forgiveness because I was told I was a sinner (aren't we all?) and saying some prayers that would get me through the week until I went to church again. It felt like a vicious cycle. I did not feel connected to God as a young person — even though I was a regular at his house.

Plus, there are a lot of mixed messages when it comes to religion, and as you get older it's not uncommon to question the validity of those messages. I mean, we all know people who go to church on the regular, and at the same time are not being very church-like outside their house of worship. We all know the controversy about certain religions denouncing human beings because of their sexuality, or here's one for ya, because they were not conceived "naturally."

Yep, I know this because a friend of mine who struggled with fertility for a long time was able to have a child thanks to medical advances. When they went to have the baby baptized, the church wouldn't do it. The religious leader stated that they would not complete the baptism because their beautiful baby was not conceived the old-fashioned way. That's pretty terrible. Imagine spending years trying to become a parent, and when you finally do, the only church or religion you've ever known for your thirty-something years on earth shuns you for having a baby conceived unconventionally. That put a very bad taste my mouth. I've struggled with religion since.

It wasn't until I became an adult, and lived on my own, that I became interested in exploring what spirituality actually meant to me. The idea that you had to go to a specific place to be connected to your God made no sense. I mean, I was told to say my prayers at night and that wasn't in church, so why couldn't I have a connection to God right from my kitchen table if I wanted? Well, it turns out I could.

Once I realized I could have a connection to my higher power from wherever, and whenever I wanted, I would say my game changed. My spirituality was no longer about sitting in a specific structure reciting words that I had learned as a child. It was about creating a deeper connection to my highest self, my surroundings and my personal beliefs. Instead of aligning myself with a specific religion, I feel more connected to Source/God/Universe through my personal spirituality. Yes, I have my own connection to source. I believe we all do.

For me, my spirituality is about being a good person, helping humanity thrive, and giving back to the people and planet that have sustained me. I don't think you have to go to church to be a spiritual person, or to have God hear you. I believe your relationship with Source/God/Universe is the same as your relationship with a friend or partner. It's deeply personal and should be treated with respect and admiration.

Having a comfortable connection with my spirituality has been a growing process. I've found that as I get older, the truth in my spirituality is that it is more internal. The more I focused on what my heart was directing me toward, the easier it became to listen to my internal voice. So often we allow outside noise and opinion dictate how we "think" we're supposed to feel, when in reality each or our relationships with our own guiding force is extremely personal. None of us could, or should have the same relationship with our God. They should all be deeply personal based on where you are in your life and what you need.

## BECAUSE... *When God Speaks, I Listen!*

I realize how ironic this next section is going to appear, especially after the last story I shared. Even though I don't necessarily have a connection to God just because I'm in church, I actually LOVE churches in real life. Especially the ones that are old and have a lot of history. When I walk into any church I feel a sense of grounded calm and appreciation. It's instant. It doesn't matter the denomination either, I'm drawn to the architecture and beauty of them. So, while I don't typically go to them during worship hours, it's not unusual that I stop into one on a random afternoon especially if it's a church I haven't seen yet, or in a while.

While I've been drawn to the architecture and beauty of churches for as long as I can remember, the deep appreciation I have for them has really only been in my adulthood. Especially when I'm reminded about how they're not always about the worship and are more about the community. A few years ago, I was meeting a friend in New York City for dinner. The restaurant we were going to just happened to be in the neighborhood where I used to live. It had been about ten years since I had lived there so I decided to go early to walk around, connect with my former streets, and check out the new places in the hood.

As I was walking, I heard music in the air. I decided to investigate where it was coming from. Lo and behold, it was coming from the historic Trinity Church, which just happens to be the church I used to look at from my living room window in lower Manhattan when we lived there. The music I heard was their choir. They were practicing for an upcoming concert. I was drawn inside, along with several other spectators to listen. I took the liberty to sit in a pew, soak in the beauty of the church, and be still.

This also happened to be a week where I was really questioning my decision to start my own business. I was feeling fragile and unsure. I needed encouragement and support, and I hadn't truly realized it until the moment I walked into that church. I sat for a good fifteen minutes, allowing myself to clear my head and ask for guidance. The choir started to sing *Amazing Grace* — one of my favorites. For me, the meaning of the song is about perseverance through grace. It means there will be bumps along the way but we should get up and move through them. It means appreciating the journey. This was exactly the sign I needed. I felt guided to it. I needed to step into that church on that night. I needed to hear those words to let me know I was making the right decisions. I needed to be reminded of grace.

My spiritual connection plays a big part in my day-to-day life. Spirit is always there for me when I need it. Because I spend time every day developing my connection to God/Source/Universe, I feel like God is there for me when I ask. From signs and symbols to manifestation and synchronicity, I know that the Universe will show up and assist me.

How do I know that the Universe will show up for me? Because I know how to ask my question, and wait for the answer. For me it's about being aware and present in the time I'm dedicating to my spiritual practice. It requires some patience. I know that if I ask for guidance, I may not get it when I want it but it will show up when I need it.

I have a few different things I do to stay centered and grounded and in connection so that I can be ready to hear my answers when it's time. I spend time connecting to my inner spirit almost every day. When I do, side benefit, I'm definitely more patient and compassionate of others.

From using it daily in everything I do with consideration and intention, to using it in my coaching and teaching my children. It certainly does come in handy! When talking about awareness and spirituality, I think my daily practice plays a significant role. It gives me the ability to get out of my head and focus on listening to my inner voice and higher guidance. Because they are so powerful, I'm sharing my most effective spiritual connection practices below. It is my sincere wish that any or all of these practices will help you in your connection to your higher power, and in your everyday life.

Gratitude practice is something I do for myself and suggest to almost all of my clients. Spending a few minutes every day when I wake up and before I go to bed, being thankful for my day, my experiences, my health and all the blessings I've been gifted with creates a deep appreciation for my life. Because as humans, it's easy to take things for granted. Practicing being thankful allows me to take out the irritations and frustrations, and step back into a loving space when I need it.

Talking to (or praying to) God and my angels is another practice I do daily. I mean, I'm the girl in the grocery store talking to herself out loud, so taking the time to talk to my spirits is not out of the ordinary for me. I ask for guidance and signs when I'm feeling like I need a lift or a little confirmation in my direction. I personally like having a connection to the Universe. I believe the Universe is listening and will communicate back in signs, symbols, ideas and downloads. Prayer allows me to connect and appreciate my relationship with God and my spirits. I really feel like I am being heard when I pray.

Having a daily ritual of meditation is something that I have come to rely on and appreciate as I move through my life. Especially as we are about to embark on the teenage years with Wyatt. With teenagers around, I feel like having a way to center myself is important. I've found meditation to be helpful in clearing my mind of the physical and energetic noise that we can get so quickly caught up in. Even if it's only for a few moments, some meditation every day really does allow me to focus on de-stressing myself, so I can be more calm and present. There are lots of videos and meditation experts out there. Agapi Stassinopoulos, Gabby Bernstein, and Abraham Hicks are some of my faves. I encourage you to explore what lights you up. I listen to a guided meditation in the morning when I drink my tea, hear the words, breathe deeply and connect with my soul. It helps with my productivity and my outlook for the day!

I find that when I'm aware of the way I'm treating myself when it comes to my spirit, I have a much higher vibe than when I neglect it. I get that spirituality and religion are deeply personal choices and beliefs. Yet you don't have to be a believer in anything to find a connection within yourself on a deeper level. Something as simple as low music in a quiet space with a lit candle can be transforming for you. But whatever it is, I highly recommend connecting with yourself every day. When you have a solid connection to, and relationship with your whole self, anything is possible.

## BECAUSE... *We Don't All Have to Believe the Same Thing!*

From a young age, I was lucky to have experienced religious diversity. While I was raised Catholic, we had friends who were Jewish, Southern Baptist and other flavors of Christianity. I even spent a few years as a member of the Baptist church youth group. Not once did I feel like I didn't belong there. I was accepted for who I was and it was appreciated that I could be open minded to want to learn from a different church than I was used to. As I got older and started exploring the world for myself, (living in different cities, traveling to new places), I became interested and enchanted with the variety of people I met and observed. I love to people watch. Before we had real responsibilities, like kids, Will and I would hang out in Union Square park on the weekends people watching. For hours. All day. People are fascinating. I'm especially captivated by the people who are there advocating for their religion's or spiritual beliefs.

The mix of religions in New York City is really like no other place on earth, it truly is amazing. We have all of the major ones including some ideologies you've probably never even heard of! Seeing the amount of diversity in one location the way I do on a daily basis has kept my awareness heightened that much of the world doesn't think exactly like I do. I find that to be a beautiful thing. Powerful thought to remember. Keeps me humble.

There's something to be said for being present in the world, believing what you believe, and also recognizing the beliefs of other people. It is so easy to think that because someone doesn't agree with you, that it takes away from your beliefs in some way.

I'm here to tell you that it most certainly doesn't. It makes you more aware and accepting of the differences of life in general. I'm forever grateful for those lazy days before we had kids and other responsibilities. Being able to sit and soak in the activities that were going on around me opened my eyes to so much diversity. Culture and mannerisms. Compassion and ignorance. Praise and punishment. Opulence and desperation. I've seen a lot.

Seeing the world — and I mean really seeing it — has given me the ability to respect and appreciate the differences between myself and others. It's certainly made me grateful that I have the opportunity to live and interact with such great diversity on a regular basis. If fact, my love for observing and listening to people has been a major catalyst for my choosing to go into coaching. Seeing people so deeply made me passionate about wanting to help others.

## BECAUSE... *Spirituality In Action!*

Like I've said, spirituality isn't only about prayer and connection to your higher power. It's also about your personal presence and how you choose to lead your life. Will you be guided by consideration and compassion or will you not? My spirituality has given me a powerful ability to be present. It has come in handy for me, especially in emergency situations. Maybe that's my superpower.

On Sept 11th, 2001 everyone's awareness was heightened for the obvious reasons. But because I had already spent time getting in tune with my higher self, it was easy for me to jump into action in my office and quickly organize a plan to get our people home (hopefully) safely. I didn't run around like Chicken Little assuming the sky was falling, even though it was quite literally. I delegated tasks. I found TV's we could watch. Turned on a radio for news. Called loved ones while the phones were still available. Things like that I'm good at.

Incredibly, I don't remember feeling fear that day until I actually spoke to Will. He was at home in our apartment, which happened to be two blocks below the World Trade Center. I was in my office in midtown Manhattan when I got a call from a co-worker in Nashville. She asked how far I was from the towers. To which I explained I wasn't close, but Will was home and he was probably leaving for work in a short while. He works for MSNBC and at that time, his office was in New Jersey so he would commute through the World Trade Center every day. I promptly hung up with my friend and called home.

Will was in the shower when I called. Our conversation went like this: phone rings, answering machine picks up. I say in a concerned voice "Hey, are you still home, can you pick up please?" over and over. He picks up, finally, and says "I'm in the shower, what's up? I'm dripping wet." At that point, I asked him to go to the window and look to his left and tell me what he saw. He did that and said to me, "Um, I have to call you back" and hung up. You could see the towers from our windows. He was watching it unfold in front of his eyes and documenting it on film while trying to stay calm and be in communication with me and his office. I can remember saying to him, "Come here now," during our last phone conversation before we lost contact.

That's all I really remember about that conversation with my husband that morning. You'd think there would be more, but we were both in shock. Will would later write about his experience that day and have his article published by NBC News. My friend Suanne was so inspired by his words that she used them in one of her books. His story is truly amazing.

For several hours, Will was stuck in our home, alone. There was no way out for him. The area was unstable. It was an extremely dangerous situation. He literally had to wait for the dust to settle, until the area was clear for him to be able to leave the building safely. We had to wait it out. We had been married for exactly 3 months and 2 weeks.

Once we lost communication there was a lot of speculating and pacing among the people still left in the office, the locals, the city dwellers. We ordered pizza from downstairs and worried together. We made lists of the people we knew who worked in the affected area, and we prayed. When Will finally walked through the doors of my office, many hours later, covered in dust, debris and who-knows-what-else mixed in, I couldn't move for a minute. I couldn't think. I was stunned... I just remember this intense wave of relief from seeing him, of having him next to me — wash over me. We cried and we hugged for a long time and I knew in that moment we would be okay. I knew that we could make it through anything.

I will say this, there was not one second during the time I was waiting for him to show up that I thought something bad had happened to him. I'm sure I said a lot of prayers that day, but I never felt like there would be a different outcome. With every fiber of my being, I knew he would walk through that door. My faith was so strong. Because I spent so much time working on my intuition, and developing my connection to source, I could feel the truth that he would be okay. This is how I put my spirituality into action in my everyday life.

## BECACUSE... *Alone Doesn't Need to Mean Lonely!*

When you're working on developing your spirituality or faith, I also recommend getting comfortable with being alone. Learn how to enjoy your own company. Does that feel easy, or difficult? If you're a social person and feel lost when you're alone, this could be a good exercise for you. Spending time with yourself can really change your own perception of yourself. We can get so wrapped up in the day-to-day stuff that we aren't allowing time to get into our own heads to really make friends with ourselves.

I used to travel a lot for work when I was in my early 20's. At first, it was difficult for me to be alone for any period of time, like keep-me-up anxiety-inducing nervousness difficulty. I would get on a plane alone, check into an unfamiliar hotel in a new unfamiliar city alone, and then have to find things to do in between meetings with clients — alone. It felt so uncomfortable! My trips were short. A day here, two days there, but they were frequent. They forced me to have to get comfortable being alone with me. I learned how to be okay with sitting in a restaurant at a table for one with a book, or some work. I learned how to stroll around unfamiliar surroundings and take advantage of learning about new places. I learned how to be more self-aware and in tune to my own personal needs. I learned a lot about myself during that time.

This of course, was back in the day before we all had these walking entertainment devices attached to the end of our arms. That experience of traveling alone forced me to break out of a semi-introverted shell and strike up conversations with strangers in random places. It forced me to find comfort within myself, and realize that being alone for short periods of time is actually a good thing. Since then I can confidently say I love spending time alone. I mean, now I have kids that suck the life out of me a lot of the time, so any time I can get that includes silence I will gladly take it! Get comfortable in your own skin. If you haven't done it, I challenge you to go out to a restaurant, shopping or even take a little trip alone. It can be good for your spirit.

## BECAUSE... *Being Of Service to Others Feels Good!*

When you have a good sense of yourself and your faith, it shows on the outside. Doing good deeds, paying it forward, and just being nice become easier the more you do it. It's not hard to be nice if you feel good. (But it can certainly feel difficult if you yourself aren't happy!) To smile at a passerby. To compliment a stranger. Sometimes those small gestures can make a person's day. Be nice. Live by the golden rule. Be an example for your world by exercising compassion, awareness, and showing love.

Being mindful of others isn't necessarily difficult, but sometimes, if we are preoccupied, being mindful isn't as obvious. It's easy in today's uber-busy world to get caught up in a situation and not even realize that we may (or may not) be offending someone else. It's also easy to get wrapped up in our own stuff, and ignore, or not even notice when someone needs us. This is not being mindful.

How many times have you walked by someone who possibly could've used a hand carrying their baby stroller up some steps, or not held the door for the person behind you? Hey, it happens. We're all guilty of it. Except here's the thing, it feels good when someone holds the door for you or helps you with a package, right? I believe you get back what you put out into the world, so why not make someone else feel good too?

I think we've lost some of the spontaneity that comes with a random act of kindness. Saying hello to a neighbor is something we could do more often. Smile at a stranger on the street, and see what happens. On occasion, be the person at the coffee shop who pays for the person behind you. Those seemingly small gestures to you can be a big deal to someone else. What can feel tiny to you could be a huge gesture of love for the receiver.

I was in the grocery store not that long ago, standing in line answering a text on my phone while waiting for the person in front of me to finish up. I felt like it had been a while, and the line was not moving. That's when I realized that he was trying to decide which items to pull out of his order. The order that included baby food, and other necessary items because he didn't have enough money. I asked him how much he was short, he said about ten dollars. I handed him the cash. He was completely shocked. Like tears to his eyes shocked. He could not thank me enough for my generosity. He even asked me for my address so he could pay me back — which I refused to give him. After he left, the cashier thanked me for being nice. I suggested that stores like the one we were in should have a slush fund for every cashier. I'm sure it happens all the time that someone is short a few dollars. Spare them the embarrassment and cover it for them. Especially when there's food for kids involved. If we all did a random act for a stranger once a week, think of the lives you could impact in a short time. Food for thought (literally).

## BECADSE... *Nothing Questions Faith Like Loss!*

It's because I have a deep sense of faith that I'm often inspired by others who have strong faith as well. Birds of a feather... I have an "Aunt" (you know, in the Italian families, everyone is an Aunt or an Uncle) who seemed to be living the fairytale life when she was young. She and my uncle were happily married. They had just bought a pretty house in New Jersey and were trying to have a baby when my aunt was diagnosed with a mass on her brain. It was operable, and thank goodness benign, however she did lose most of her hearing in that ear. After that she became pregnant with their first child. It was the early 80's so the ultrasound was basically new and genetic testing was non-existent. When she delivered her baby boy it was discovered that he had Down Syndrome and two holes in his heart. The doctors didn't think he would make it past a few days. He ultimately survived for just under a year, passing away in her arms as she held him. I can't imagine the feeling of losing a child. While I know a few people who have experienced it, I will never be able to grasp it.

After the loss of their son, my uncle was diagnosed with cancer. He required a bone marrow operation that in those days was only done in a few hospitals in all of the United States. He went to Seattle to have his. It was successful and for a short time he was in remission. It was enough time to welcome a daughter into their family, but not enough to watch her grow into the super successful woman she is today. He passed away when she was just two years old.

Reeling from the loss of a child AND a spouse while you have a toddler is unfathomable to me. My aunt was able to climb out of this abyss, albeit with some difficulty. But, she did it. She was able to lean in to her faith to find love again. She did this through the group she attended for widowed partners. Her now husband had a similar story. He lost his wife and his son. Their experiences bonded them.

They've both done so much healing. When I see them, we spend our time laughing and enjoying each other's company. They are now at a point in their lives where they have retired and are spending time on themselves. Traveling, seeing friends and living.

They are both a testament to how you can choose to live with your faith. They both did some serious work and healing on themselves to keep believing that there is still good to be had after so much loss and tragedy. They both believe that their faith helped them through their dark times. They leaned on their family and friends and focused on raising their remaining children. They made conscious efforts to continue to find happiness and move on. And at the same time, they are generous with their friends and loved ones and have managed to stay mindful of their stories and of themselves throughout their lives. I'm inspired by them and reminded after our visits that we always have a choice when it comes to the way we want to live.

I realize not everyone experiences the level of tragedy that my aunt and uncle went through. While we all face different trials and challenges in our lives, it's the way we CHOOSE to address them that makes the difference. They both chose to embrace their faith as a way to get through it. Being able to stand strongly in your beliefs includes being kind, generous and compassionate even when it feels difficult. My aunt and uncle are a shining example of that for me.

*Finding a connection to a spiritual source is comforting. It doesn't matter what you believe when it comes to spirituality. It only matters that you have an outlet that helps you find inner peace. Being in sync with your spirit can bring you joy, and it can affirm for you that faith is something uniquely individual to each of us. Don't be afraid to connect with your belief if it helps you achieve tranquility.*

## BECAUSE... *All the Love!*

Woo Hoo! You've officially made it through the loving yourself part of this book! In this section we've explored the holistic ideas of self-love (mind, body and spirit). We've unpacked a lot of food for thought and I've shared my personal stories with the hope that you might have resonated with my learnings and lessons. I said it at the beginning of this book, and I'll say it again, the most important relationship you'll ever have is the one with yourself. I truly hope you believe that now more than ever. If you haven't already, I hope that you begin to make yourself a priority.

# PART TWO

# Relationships with Others

Cultivating a relationship with someone else isn't easy. There are a lot of factors that come into play along with a lot of feelings that need tending to. Every one of our relationships requires work. And in true hard work fashion, the more you put in to it, the more you get out of it. In these next chapters, we're going to explore all of the relationships we encounter in our lives from family to friends and everything in between including the ones we've lost along the way. We're going to learn why each one of our relationships is important and how to continue to make them thrive — without all of the yelling.

## BECAUSE...

# *Relationships & Growing Up!*

You know, the years between the ages of 11 - 19 are probably the most difficult to get through for a human being. And here's why: you're stupid. Literally. I'm not trying to insult. It's because your brain isn't fully developed according to science (There's a great article on *Live Science* that talks about the development of the adolescent brain — I highly recommend you check it out. https://www.livescience.com/13850-10-facts-parent-teen-brain.html). During these years, the adolescent brain is busy working hard and evolving into a smarter, adult brain.

The irony is, when you're in that phase, you think you know everything. This by the way, could not be further from reality. At this stage, you know basically nothing, and yet somehow you make it through. This is the time where we do the most growth — physically, hormonally, emotionally and mentally. All at the same time! The adolescent years are the ones where we're trying to figure out who we are. We experiment with our boundaries. We are growing our communication skills, and we have no idea how to handle our bodies (boobs, anyone?)

I mean, don't you remember what being a teenager was like? I absolutely do. Don't get me wrong, it's not all bad. I've got more good memories from those years than bad, but they were not without challenge.

Being a kid is hard. Trying to work through all of the changes and challenges while also maintaining some semblance of coolness with those around you is not an easy feat. This section is dedicated to the years of confusion, exploration, insecurity and seemingly never -ending emotion. I want to talk about the growth that happens during these very formative years and how these moments can help to make, or break, the relationships in our lives. Typically, we emerge from these years without really understanding just how they truly impact the way we view relationships. Because these years do so much to shape dealing with others later on, I knew I had to start here in this book.

Adolescence is all part of growing up. It comes with a mixed bag of shit. Learning how to work through our own bag and look back on it with a more mature set of eyes will only help us create better relationships now for ourselves. And if you are a parent, for your kids too. We'll be looking through that set of eyes from this spot forward at some of the most significant types of relationships. Almost all of them.

Here's how I see it, these are the years where we really learned how to create and understand relationships. We had time as youngsters to watch and learn from the big people in our lives. Our parents, teachers, coaches, neighbors and family showed us how they cultivated and treated their relationships and for the most part, we emulated them.

Relationships take on new meanings when we hit our adolescent years. Feelings arise that we've never experienced before. These feelings will run from exciting to confusing to upsetting, and every emotion in between. Romance, intimacy, and vulnerability are all new to our experience in these slightly more adult years. This is also, typically, the time we go from sharing everything with our parents to becoming guarded about certain subjects.

Given that we agree that these years are no walk in the park, let's use some of the biggest lessons I've learned to help make our relationships better today.

# BECAUSE... *Feelings Get Hurt!*

When you're a small child, ideally your early years are spent playing, feeling safe, being loved and having fun. I don't recall much at this age, except how it felt to be mistreated by others. I mean, none of us is immune to the memory of not being picked to be part of the team we wanted to be on, or having a friend tell you you're not invited to the party. If you are reading this it's likely that you've been both the giver and receiver of those experiences. It happens early. I know in our family, my boys have both come home with hurt feelings because a friend said something that was not nice to one of them, or didn't include them, or teased them for one thing or another.

I don't remember how my parents handled these things, but I can tell you how I do. I give my children the power and space to express their feelings when they're upset. I allow them to cry or be mad because their feelings have been hurt. I allow them time to really think about how that feels and then I ask them to tell me how they want to respond. A lot of times, kids are not equipped with the knowledge of knowing how to respond to unkind remarks. They're often taken off guard and don't have the capacity to deal with the situation without wanting to shut down, run away, or fight.

As much as we try to prepare our children, we can't expect them to behave the way an adult would. We know how we would handle a situation like that, but I'm pretty sure when we were kids, we didn't. I want to make sure if (when) an uncomfortable situation happens again, they're prepared with a proper response.

Now don't get me wrong, the mama bear inside me wants to grab anyone that hurts my kid by the collar and give them a good shake, but the calm and rational mama that I am knows that's not the answer. I encourage my kids to find a way to express themselves firmly without causing any more insult or pain. The right thing to do for my boys is to tell their friends how they feel when they're uncomfortable or are being mistreated. A response to your friend, "So-and-so, you're hurting my feelings." Or, "That's not nice," is a good start. A lot of times, kids, especially the little ones, don't always realize they're hurting someone else's feelings. Oftentimes the young ones aren't doing it maliciously, they just haven't developed their filters yet. It's the bigger ones you have to watch out for.

Let's be honest, it doesn't feel good to have your feelings hurt. Building awareness with our kids is the first line of defense. Teaching them the obvious things like kindness, consideration and empathy are important. And letting them know that they can and should use their voices to express their feelings is a good place to start. I often remind my children to choose their words wisely because they can't be taken back. And to remember that just because their feelings may have gotten hurt, it doesn't mean they get to retaliate in an unkind way.

Adolescence is very different from the elementary years because we now have the ability to really begin to explore the power of our voice and how to use it in our relationships. We are testing the water with our ideas and opinions and in some cases, looking for reactions from our friends, family and other adults. We are uncovering the truth about ourselves and our expectations. Because, especially in this day and age, children are encouraged to be heard. We are teaching them how to be better communicators at earlier ages than ever before, and to do so with lots of love and respect.

## BECAUSE... *Everyone's Opinion Matters!*

I'm dating myself here, but back in the day when I was growing up, feelings and emotions weren't really discussed. I mean, I can recall being told to stop crying as my mother went about doing whatever it was she was doing, most likely cleaning something, as opposed to being validated. Parents weren't taught to stop what they were doing to talk about, and validate kid emotions. We never discussed why I was having upset feelings, and how I could learn how to remedy the situation.

Our opinions weren't requested by our parents either. I'm not putting my parents down. This is the way it was with everyone's family around me. Parents made family decisions without talking to the kids about it. We were told later what would happen next. Now, I'm not saying we need to involve our kids in all of our decisions. If we did that at my house, we would be living in a treehouse, eating junk food and playing video games all day long. But, I do think there's a positive and empowering outcome when it comes to including your children in discussions that will ultimately affect their lives, like, perhaps moving to a different state. I was just shy of my twelfth birthday when we moved from the suburbs of New York City to Florida. You wanna talk about life change? Honey, pull up a chair.

Imagine taking a uniform wearing, Catholic school girl out of the rolling-hilled, tree-lined-streets-full-of-bik e-riding-kids-with-scraped-knees New York suburbs, and dropping her in the twilight zone known as rural, coastal Florida. That was me. It was a completely different world. And by that I mean that it was flat, humid, there were no kids to play with, and only retirees for neighbors. Florida really did feel like *The Twilight Zone.*

What happened to our beautiful street filled with great neighbors and tons of kids to play with? What's this place you call public school?

Where's my uniform?!

"WHYAREYOUDOINGTHISTOME?" I would cry to my mother.

"It's an adjustment for all of us. You'll be fine," she would tell me.

When my parents decided to move to Florida, I don't recall there being any family discussion about it. We were simply told this was happening. Deal with it. Now that I'm a parent, I realize the importance of communication around family decisions. I'm not saying that we should let the kids make the decisions, I'm simply suggesting that they be included in the discussion.

We do a lot of communicating with our kids in our home. We ask for their opinions and discuss options on everything from our daily schedules to vacation ideas. We allow them to weigh in on their educational choices. And yes, we even let them have an opinion when we bought our home. It's my belief that if you include your kids in the discussions at a younger age, they are going to be good at initiating good communication as they grow up.

Something as big as a move to a different state, where we basically knew no one, is something that would garner a family discussion in my home. But times were different back when I was a young-ster. We just went along for the ride.

Now don't get me wrong. My childhood tragedies could have been worse. Sure. I can easily say this 30-some odd years later. But at the time, in the moment, it was the worst thing on the planet for me. It wasn't that great for my little brother either. Although he did end up making Florida his home, and still lives there to this day.

At the time, it was hard to adjust to not having friends when we had so many at our disposal in our old neighborhood — at any time of the day. Instead of going out to play with friends after school, we hung out inside watching TV because no friends lived close by. Back in my day we didn't have things like organized playdates and welcome committees like they do now. There weren't places to go to meet new people other than church. We did have some friends from New York who made the move to the same town in Florida that we did, which was a bit of a cushion to the blow, but because we no longer lived on the same street, we were relegated to seeing them only on weekends and at school.

It was hard enough being a tweenager, then throw a new loca-tion, no friends, and new school into the mix. It was a recipe for internal chaos. It was a really tough time for me. Because of my experience, and the lack of communication around it, I'm hell-bent on keeping the lines of communication open with my kids. It helps to keep their internal chaos to a minimum.

## BECAUSE... *Will You Accept Me For Me??*

I know we talked about body love earlier in the book, but that was more of an overview on a personal level. In this section, I want to talk about the awkwardness of acceptance — especially when it relates to being a teen.

Acceptance is such an important part of growing up. How do we fit in? Why is it so hard to feel accepted? What about the pressure of trying to be one of the "cool kids?" That pressure of acceptance is so strong, and affects our relationships so much — even as adults — that I've decided we've got to talk about it.

All any of us really wants is to be accepted and to fit in with our peers, no matter what age we are. As I was thinking about how I was going to write this section, two things came up for me:

First, there's "how do I look" with regard to superficial acceptance like the hair, clothes, etc. This also encompasses all of the physical body changes that can make us feel vulnerable, and awkward.

Then there's the, "how do I look" in terms of what's actually going on inside of us. The emotions, the tension, and the deep desire to want to be liked so badly, that you are willing to compromise what you believe in order to be "cool." Those trade-offs for acceptance start to happen early, and can affect how you treat yourself and others for the rest of your life.

Dealing with both simultaneously is so damn confusing! Like, "Does this shirt look ok with these jeans? And, "Why is he/she being so mean to me? It must be because of me wearing these jeans," all in the same thought... Sheesh, growing up can feel exhausting!

Let's discuss getting accepted for your appearance/body first. Will we ever stop obsessing about how we look during our lifetime? For something that we have little control over like the way we are born, it surprising this is still an issue. For most of us, I'm gonna go out on a limb and say no, we probably won't stop.

I'm pretty sure everyone I know has wondered on uncountable numbers of occasions if they look okay-good-nice-hot-awesome-fat-ugly. That's because you are surrounded by billboards, advertisements, commercials, peers and others that keep you focused on how you look to others. Not much time is spent on how you look and feel about yourself. While I know we as a society are starting to shift back to loving what you've been given, it wasn't always that way.

When I was a kid, and especially after we moved to another state, I worried about having the right clothes, shoes, accessories, haircut, bag and on and on and on. I didn't want to be made fun of if I didn't have the latest fashion brand of jeans. I was completely worried that I wouldn't fit in.

I remember a particular instance when I did not feel accepted, and it was because of my clothes, which seems ridiculous now. But, at the time, it felt life-ending. It was my first day, at my new school in Florida, 1984. I no longer had to wear a uniform and I could choose basically anything I wanted to wear to school. I remember being nervous about having to make new friends. I was scared about going to a much larger school. I had no idea what to expect. This created some anxiety about being the new girl. What's hilarious is that I had no idea how to dress for public school. If you remember, I went to private school up until this point. I didn't have to choose any clothes on a daily basis. They were chosen for me.

I remember being so excited that I had the opportunity to choose an outfit that had some character, but I chose something close to what I knew. I wore a white tee style shirt with little pearls sewn on the front, a wide check plaid skirt that resembled a tablecloth, in grey and white that touched my ankles, and grey Nine West ballet flats with a bow on the front. I looked like a Catholic school girl. As soon as I got to school, and saw what the other kids were wearing, I was terrified that I would stand out like a sore thumb. What did I do? How would I fit in now?!?

I worried, stressed and tried to gauge the reactions of the students around me. Had I had made the right choice? Would the kids at my new school make fun of my outfit? Would I be accepted? Would I fit in? How would I know if they actually liked me?

Thankfully no one made fun of me or caused me any particular angst, but I do remember feeling a little...square. As soon as I got to school, I quickly realized that my style needed a little infusion of fun and youth. At this school I would have the freedom to be less buttoned up and more trendy. It seemed that the social judgment wasn't as strong at this school either. The kids were relaxed and more open. While I basically got out of my first day unscathed, it wasn't lost on me how hard it is for us, especially during our adolescent years, to feel like we fit in.

As soon as I got the fashion part dealt with, that emotional pressure I was talking about earlier started to move in. It's during this weird developmental time, that we start caring about how other people perceive us. If you thought choosing the right clothing to be accepted was stressful, this is a whole new level of intensity. How will I find my people? What is it about me that people actually like? What do I do if I feel like I can't handle the peer pressure?

I was recently having a conversation with a friend about wanting to fit in when you're in new surroundings and how a lot of kids will give into peer pressure in order to do so. Their child had just bumped into that. This happens a lot around the time we head off to college. Nerves are heightened, our parents are far away, we don't have a lot of guidance and we are expected to make decisions for ourselves on a more mature level. If we're not ready for that, the outcome could be a complete disaster.

Case in point, my client has a daughter who went away to school and seemingly had a great freshman year. For some reason, her return home for summer break found her racked with anxiety and the idea that she was physically sick. Like most of us when we were of college age, she was nervous about fitting in and making friends so she gave in when it came to being exposed to new things like experimenting with drugs. In this particular situation, she made the choice to try something she had never done before and the effects of it scared the living daylights out of her. So much so that she was having a hard time trusting her judgement and was questioning her personal strength.

The changes in her demeanor left her family concerned which lead to her parents asking a ton of questions she didn't want to have to answer. This caused a major panic attack which ended in a trip to the emergency room. Once she was there, and because she's an adult, she was able to talk to the doctors and come clean about her personal situation.

It seems that she made a few questionable decisions while she was away at school which led her to being in one particular situation where she ended up passing out and not knowing where she was when she came to. Thank goodness she was with friends and they had looked out for her. While that was helpful, it did not reduce her fear and newfound anxiety.

Since her experience, she has been feeling like she let her parents down. She's nervous about going back to school, and she's terrified that something bad will happen to her again. This is all because she wanted to fit in with her new crowd. She wanted so badly to be accepted. Her parents are doing all they can to make sure they have the whole story so they can help her.

Many of us have been there, in a questionable situation in front of our friends, not sure how to proceed because we are afraid of being uncool. We see it happen every day. Kids, and adults, succumbing to peer pressure for fear of not being accepted. So how do we change it?

As a parent, this is one of my biggest fears. That my children would put themselves at risk in order to be accepted. Will and I work so hard to create open dialogue with our kids, encouraging them to communicate no matter what the subject. Acceptance is a hard topic to navigate. In the case of my client's daughter, we're working through getting her to feel well enough to stand on her own two feet, gain her confidence back and learn from her experience. Her overall health and safety is what's truly important here.

It's only human nature to want to be accepted no matter what stage of life you're in. Remember, you'll never be accepted for who you are until you accept yourself first.

I used to easily fall into the trap of "Keeping Up with the Joneses" as a way to feel accepted, even though I know it's a terrible way to create friendships. Living a life that's inauthentic is hard to maintain. Every time I've done it in the past it's been stressful. If I can't be myself around my people, then I'm not with the right people. Once I realized that, the weight lifted and I could begin to live the life I was meant to live. At the end of the day it really doesn't matter who has the most toys — it matters how I created and sustained long lasting successful relationships in my life.

## BECAUSE... *Friends Make It Bearable!*

Now that we've talked about acceptance, let's chat about the insecurities around the intense physical developmental time of adolescence, and how sometimes, those insecurities actually bring us closer together. Kids aren't only worried about how they look with regard to the clothes they wear, they obsess about how their bodies look too. Finding comfort in your own skin can take time — so having friends around to support you through it is what really makes it bearable.

What's important here, is to let your kids know they're not alone in the awkward feelings department. When I was a kid, it was definitely my friends that helped me through the weird and uncomfortable stages of physical development. It was an opportunity to bond over and learn from one another as we each tried to navigate this extremely important time in our lives.

It was bad enough that I was trying to find my footing, let alone having to learn how to deal with my new body. And I wasn't alone in those feelings. My friends were going through it too, thank goodness! Bra shopping anyone? Let's just say there wasn't Victoria's Secret in the mall back then. There were sections in department stores that said **Training Bras** on a huge sign overhead (facepalm). Who wants to stand there — with their MOM — in that section?? The embarrassment was unavoidable. What exactly *were* we training for with those bras?

And why-oh-why was it such a big deal to get your period? WHY did my mother have to call EVERYONE she knows to tell them? I think my grandparents gave me $20 bucks in a congratulations card when they found out I was "Officially a Woman." What the hell?? OMG!! Mortifying!! We did not discuss those things in our family!

It wasn't until I was at a beach party with a bunch of friends that I learned how to actually use a tampon. Thank goodness for my friends who made it all better! I can clearly remember being in my friend's bedroom, on my period, not wanting to change into my bathing suit and she was like, "just use a tampon." This, of course, started the discussion and encouragement of all of my girlfriends about how to use one, and how it would change my life. So, off I went, armed with a few of them, just in case I did it wrong the first time. I did not, just for the record. At that moment, my life was changed. I was free! Sheesh, the things you remember.

Alls I'm saying is — Thank God For My Friends!

## BECAUSE... *Bullies!*

It's hard enough having to deal with our own insecurities as kids. Having others call it out is even worse. Bullying is terrible and should have no place in the world, but unfortunately, that's not realistic. Arming our children with the tools they need (and the ones we wish we had when we were younger) is beyond important today. I decided to talk about bullying because it is a relationship situation that happens to many of us when we are young. Whether you were the bully, or the bullied, this activity can have lasting and profound effects in our relationships.

I have a friend who moved to Florida from New Jersey when we were in high school. His parents relocated in part because of a situation where he was bullied in his former school. When we were kids, I had no idea he had been through any kind of ordeal, let alone the magnitude of it. It has only been recently that he decided to bring it to light. It's still something that affects his self-esteem.

After my friend decided to be open about his experience, he contacted some of his old friends from his New Jersey school to share his story. He was comforted to know that he wasn't alone in his feelings. Other kids, during the same time period, had been bullied as well. They now appreciated him speaking up about it. He told me he's been in contact with several of his former classmates. They have had deep conversations about their difficult time. Each of them has had to come to terms with their situations differently and twenty something years later, are trying to find peace with it.

It's hard enough dealing with bullying when you're a kid, but when it's YOUR kid who's being bullied, well, that's a whole different ball game. I was recently talking with one of my clients and she was telling me about her son who's having a difficult time of it with a bullying friend lately.

Her son is ten years old. He hasn't hit his growth spurt yet, so he's currently a bit "husky." Apparently, a friend of his likes to point it out every chance he gets. This teasing has been causing all kinds of issues between the boys. All my client wants to do is protect her son. What's most shocking to me is that these boys have been friends since they were babies. How could they treat each other poorly? While I'm no stranger to kids being mean to one another, I've never witnessed my own children being teased maliciously by a friend.

When it hits so close to home you have to handle it with kid gloves. As I was chatting with my client I said to her, "Look at who he's learning from. His parents are known arguers. We've all seen them disrespect one another in public. Of course, this will in turn rub off onto their kids. Their kids think it's ok to treat others unkindly, and are now being labeled as bullies." It's a crappy situation, but one that can be remedied with some attention, love and intent.

After talking it through, I advised her that the way to address it is two-fold. First, the parents need to chat. Heart to heart. The adults need to come to an understanding about the situation, and how to resolve it. I'm sure that once a true discussion is had there will be steps taken to repair any damage. If not, these people are not your people. A decision to change the course of your relationship is warranted. Then, talk with the kids themselves. My client's son needs to tell his friend to stop being mean and hurtful. He has to do it in a heartfelt way by telling his friend that if he values their friendship, then he wouldn't be saying mean things.

Discovering how great you are as an individual, despite what anyone else may say, or even think, is what makes each of us more resilient. Once you understand to the core of your being what makes you special, no one else's opinion really matters. Yes, we all have "flaws" depending on how you look at them. A bully may even tease you about them. But there is a point in healthy self-esteem where opinions bounce back like rubber, instead of sticking like glue. Sound familiar?

I can look in the mirror all day long and find something "wrong" with me — a wrinkle here, grey hair there, jiggly thighs. It's all part of aging — at least that's what I tell myself. I'm trying to do it as gracefully as I can. All of those "things" tell your story. They're your book so to speak. Every scar, every line, every mark is yours and yours alone. That's a powerful thought when you take a minute to digest it.

In recent years bullying, mental health, and physical health have become major topics of discussion amongst teachers and parents. Kids learn about anti-bullying in school. We never had that. Back when I was in school, bullying wasn't labeled. To my knowledge it wasn't blatant. I don't recall kids being made fun of or being harassed in our hallways at school. That could be because I was too busy in the Student Government classroom with my friends. These days you can see it on the street with some kids, the way they treat one another and the way they treat strangers.

Then there's the whole cyber-bullying thing. That stuff is out of control once you start to educate yourself about it. Kids are creating "secret" accounts on social media just so they can troll other kids and be mean to them. WHAT? I mean come on you guys, I cannot even believe this happens. Education around the topic of bullying has become more mainstream, and I think it's a great thing, but there has to be more. That's why we're discussing it here.

I've also created a program for teenagers about knowing how to accept, embrace and create change in their lives. It gives them a leg up on how to deal with negativity and bullying and also teaches them how to control their mindset and communication to effectively turn a negative situation into a positive one. Let's build each other up instead of tear each other down. Every human on the planet needs this information.

## BECAUSE... *Healthy Boundaries!*

When I have a solid understanding about how to manage my own needs and feelings, I'm creating a healthy set of boundaries for myself. I know what I will and will not tolerate for myself and my relationships. I feel confident in the choices I make about the activities I participate in and the friendships I build. Boundaries aren't only about saying no when it comes to unhealthy situations like bullying and drugs, they're about creating a solid level of self-love and self- confidence. You're teaching yourself about self-worth which, as you know in my book, is numero uno.

Boundaries can feel difficult to put in place — especially if you haven't been doing it. There's that tricky guilt again. But because we're human, and are prone to our perfect imperfection, it might take a few tries to get new boundaries in place. That's okay. Do it anyway.

I can remember my boundaries being tested as a teenager, at parties and not wanting to partake in some of the activities that were going on. Ahem, drugs. I remember the first time that I saw pot at a party. I was with my squad and there were people and beer everywhere. We walked into the backyard, and I could smell it right away. Oh boy. One of the guys had some, and of course offered it. And there I was...in the moment. What choice would I make? Would I risk getting in trouble? Would it even be worth it?

Maybe it was because my parents were heavy cigarette smokers when I was a kid, and I was frequently tortured by their second-hand smoke. Perhaps it was because my parents used to threaten our lives if we ever tried to smoke or do drugs. Maybe my subconscious was protecting me from their wrath?

At any rate, I just knew in my gut that it wasn't for me. I never really felt pressured into trying something I was adamant about not wanting either. I just naturally had strong boundaries here. I just realized early on that I don't like being completely out of control in an altered state. Disclaimer: I'm not an angel, nor do I claim to be, so for me to sit here and say I've never actually been in an altered state would be ridiculous. I just stuck to the booze and nothing else. So now you know a forty-something year old woman who has never smoked a joint or snorted a line in her life. Ever. I'm a bit of a type A control freak, so for me it doesn't feel good to give up the reins to something so uncontrollable.

While it's good to know your limits around what you'll entertain when you're out and about, it's essential to know what your limits are within your relationships. A lot of times, we have to learn this the hard way. We want so badly to fit in with certain people that we are willing to put up with being treated poorly or giving into temptation. That breaking of our boundaries ultimately makes us feel yucky.

Whether you realize it or not, exercising healthy boundaries is something we do all day, every day. You are making choices for yourself again and again. From how you allow people to talk to and behave with you, to how you treat yourself and others, you are constantly making micro choices about what you will and will not accept into your life.

## BECAUSE... *It's Changed Since I Was a Kid!*

We're not living in the stone ages anymore people. The way we communicate has changed through the years and because of that, learning how to do it properly in our relationships now can sometimes feel tricky. We didn't communicate with one another, like we do now, when I was growing up.

When I was an adolescent kid, communication was, "How was your day?" without further inquisition. This brevity worked for me, because I was at a point in my life where I craved more privacy. I closed the door to my bedroom. I tried to find quiet places to brood over the most recent thing I was mad about. I wanted want to be left alone.

Conversely, I also wanted to be surrounded by my friends, be invited to the parties and not have to deal with any pushback from my parents. When I hit the puberty stage, I clammed up, so to speak, and only divulged bits and pieces of information I thought was relevant to the situation. What was I so afraid of when I was a teenager? Not getting my way? Being judged? Offending someone? Being found out?

I mean, I can remember being a teenager and wanting to go to the party of the week and not feeling comfortable enough to ask my parents if I could go so I would make arrangements to sleep over a friend's house in order to go to said party. All of my friends did the same thing — we just had to coordinate where the sleepover was happening! Because no one really inquired, it was so easy. Luckily, none of us ever got hurt or in any trouble when we were kids, but in hindsight, I can see why it would've been smarter to be honest with our parents by asking permission to go to the parties. The trust level of communication is important in all of our relationships and even though sometimes we may not be allowed to do the things we want to do, being honest is always the best way to go.

These days our kids can't really get away with shit. There is no way they aren't communicating with us about where they are and what they're doing. Thanks to the technology devices we all carry around, our kids can now be tracked and monitored twenty-four hours a day.

All of these forms of communication are so different from when I was a kid. I mean, back in the day we didn't have our own pocket phones that allowed us to stay in constant communication with our squad. As adults we have to be careful when we're setting the example for our kids in terms of how they use their devices to communicate.

Here's how different it is now. A few years ago, Wyatt got a technology device to keep with him, his first cell phone. It was in anticipation of his moving up to middle school in Brooklyn and commuting by himself back-and-forth to school on the city bus. Basically, his father and I thought it was time for him to be tracked. Thank God tracking devices did not exist when I was a kid!

Let me just say this: we did not go into the decision of giving our then 10 year-old a phone lightly. This decision was discussed and well thought out. We finally decided that since we live where we do, the pros outweighed the cons in our specific circumstance.

We live in New York City. When kids here go to middle and high school, transportation is provided to them via the NYC transit system, either the bus or the subway. They do not have access to the yellow school buses so many of us used to ride as children. The decision to give him a phone was actually a purely selfish one for us as parents. Even though I'm sure he's responsible enough to get to school and home on his own without one. For us it's not about his ability and more about everyone else around him. Now, I realize the odds are small that something will happen to him, but on the off chance that he needs to get in touch, well, we feel better knowing he can. If we lived anywhere else in the country, we would probably have waited until he was 12 to give him a phone.

So, based on our decision, off I went to the phone store to upgrade my phone and hand the old one down to him. The giving of the phone was done intentionally and unceremoniously. He got a talk about responsibility and privilege. He was reminded that the phone he has in his possession in reality belongs to his father and I. We are allowing him to use it. He is not to download apps without permission. He is fully aware that at any time, either parent can audit his texts and phone log. He was totally fine with our list of rules. All he wanted to do was hunt Pokemon.

Of course we were nervous about giving him the gift of unlimited access to all the things a phone can bring at such an early age. Will and I went back and forth in discussion about parental restrictions, app allowances (or not) and all kinds of not-so-great scenarios Wyatt could possibly get into once he got his phone. Like I said, we did not have pocket communication devices as children, so this was totally uncharted water for us. I mean, I got my first cell phone when I was 20 years old, and it was a Motorola bag phone that plugged into the cigarette lighter of my car. No way I could carry that around. Then there was that Beeper/Pager craze. We recently found one from the late nineties that we had kept for posterity! I'm not sure why, but its in a junk drawer. When we explained the Beeper to the kids, they were dumbfounded that you actually had to call a number to have your hip vibrate to call back. Anyway, once we got over the nerves and basically talked ourselves into Wyatt's responsibility threshold, we gave in. Now he has his own phone.

Here's when the communication now, with all of this tech, gets a little trickier. About a week into him having his own device, I decided to do a random check of text messages. A few from his guy friends, "Meet at the lake." "Bring a tennis racquet." That kind of stuff. Totally harmless. Then there were the ones from the girls. In typical girl fashion, a lot of lines from her to the tune of "I like you, do you like me?" or "I know you like so and so. I'm going to tell her." That immature nonsense. What made me chuckle was the 5 lines of girl chatter and one line from him, "What?" His were one-word answers and hers were sentences.

I mean my son was 10, and this girl that was texting him was 12. What?! Big difference in maturity (you would think). She was the one talking to him about wanting to kiss him. UM...excuse me?! I thought I would die. I really did. She told him to meet her at her secret spot at the lake. Wait, what? Secret spot? Seriously? I'm not ready for this!!! Except, well, I am.

I couldn't let this just slide, so I decided to ask him what that particular conversation was about. He was not offended that I saw it and was very matter of fact about it. "Mom, I don't know what she's talking about with a secret spot at the lake. I don't want to kiss her. That's gross! I don't like her in that way. She's a little crazy." (Phew!) Good talk. But seriously, at least he's comfortable enough to know we will be checking his activity and he's not hiding anything (yet).

Communication can be scary for an adolescent kid. Especially when you are new to it. Having to admit feelings and actions to someone else can be intimidating and uncomfortable. I know my biggest learning lesson from my adolescent years with regard to communication has been that I should've been more vocal about how I was feeling in certain situations. That there was absolutely no reason to feel embarrassed or unworthy of a particular feeling I was having. That's why I'm so hell bent on making sure the lines of communication are wide open for my kids. No subject is off limits, no questions unanswered. Having them feel comfortable broaching any subject with us without judgement is what's most important, because the next phases of adolescence are right around the corner and they include some sensitive subjects.

## BECAUSE... *First Crushes!*

Do you remember the first time you found out someone had a crush on you? (raising my hand) I do. I can see the day vividly. I'm at my ballet recital, I'm in sixth grade, 11 years old. I'm wearing a lavender tutu, full performance makeup, waiting with my class to go on to wow our parents. My friend said to me "Jeff is outside. He wants to say hi. He likes you." Wait, what? Who? Jeff? He's in the seventh grade! He likes ME? That's all I remember. I don't remember if I spoke with him. I don't remember if we had any interaction after that at school. Nothing. Nada. That's all I remember. I had this memory recently and I'm sure it's because my son is experiencing some of this in his life right now. Times have changed but the general makeup of the situations remain similar.

Here's the crazy thing though — I don't actually remember MY first crush. But I do remember having crushes in general. Even to this day. I mean, what middle aged woman on the planet doesn't have a crush on George Clooney?

Adolescent crushes are a rite of passage. They're sweet and unexpected. They're the catalyst to the next level of exploring. They bring fits of giggles and racing hearts. They confirm for us that we are desirable to another human being in a more-than-friends kind of way, causing us to get all tingly and warm inside. Yeah, they're a big deal. And they should be treated as such.

They're also fraught with emotions. Just because you have a crush on someone does not mean they are crushing on you in return. How many times have you liked someone only to find out the feeling wasn't mutual? I would venture to say a few. How nervous did you feel when you made a confession to your friends that you liked someone? It's scary! We're in uncharted waters seeking the validation of a potential suitor, which is sometimes met with positive results and other times not so much. For many of us, somewhere along the way there comes some kind of teasing. You know what I'm talking about. You see a boy, you think he's cute. You tell your pack of friends how you feel only to be met with reactions like, "You're not pretty enough for him" or "Why on earth do you think he would like you?" What you thought was going to be an experience full of confirmation, excitement and love turns out to be exactly the opposite. Ego shattered. Heart Broken.

I can remember liking boys and having my dad, my brother or even my friends tease me about it. They would do things like make kissy noises and sing the *K-I-S-S-I-N-G* song. Ugh, so embarrassing. Our family and friends may think it's all in good fun, and yet it doesn't feel that way. It's bad enough when you're an adolescent kid trying to comprehend all of your new emotions, but when you feel vulnerable, and are only met with teasing by people who are supposed to be your greatest supporters, it brings up feelings of inadequacy and internal questioning. At this vulnerable stage in our lives, we could very easily buy into the idea that we're not good enough or attractive enough to be liked by someone seemingly "out of our league." I hope you realize this is complete and utter bullshit.

I get that the teasing in my case was meant to be lighthearted and jokey. I get that there are people in the world that don't think before they speak, especially when we're kids. I'm not so

117

fragile to fall into the trap of, "you're not good enough." There are people, especially adolescent youngsters, who aren't as strong as I was. Some of us live for the approval of others and when that approval is not verified, it can be heartbreaking. When you look at the situation from all points of view, it can be eye opening. A lot of times the culprit doesn't think they're doing anything wrong, but if their actions are not confronted, then the pattern will continue. IF you don't communicate back with the people who are hurting your feelings, you're not exercising the healthy boundaries I was talking about earlier in the book. In my situation, I learned that it was my job to communicate my feelings even if it felt scary.

This stuff doesn't stop as we get older either. Whether we're going through it ourselves or navigating through it with our own adolescent children it's complicated. As parents we don't want to make the wrong move! Playing it down says we don't care enough and playing it up could cause embarrassment with our kids. There's a sweet spot here — and as far as I can see, it's called playing it cool. Again, because these years are so formidable when it comes to the beginning stages of exploring our sexuality, being able to relate to our kids is one of the best ways I've learned how to handle these types of situations. Tell your kids about your first crushes. Let them know their feelings are perfectly normal and that it's cool to be curious. Do not tease them or cause them to feel like they're unworthy of the person they're crushing on. I mean, don't get me wrong, a little cutesy comment can be funny, but before you decide to

make kissy faces at your hormonal emotion bag of a kid, make sure you're doing it in the right context. I have a kid who's sensitive and serious and if I tease him when he's not in the mood for it — well then, I can expect Mr. Moody to be out in full force for a few hours. If on the other hand, he's in a playful fun mood, then I can be a little more casual and playful myself. My point being, know your audience and respect them because first crushes don't last long and the next phase (dating) is right around the corner. And that my friends will cause you to get grey hair.

# BECAUSE... *The SEX TALK!*

It's only natural for a dating relationship to lead to more intimacy (or as my adolescent friends referred to it back in the day, "doing the deed"). I don't know about you, but I was not fully prepared for the sex stuff in real life. Mostly because I wasn't very prepared for it on paper. What I mean is that my education about sex was extremely limited and quite honestly, discouraged. I'm not going to chat about my personal experiences with sex, because that's private, but I will talk about my very interesting education about it. Once upon a time, way back in the stone ages, when I was growing up, having The Sex Talk was a completely different experience than what it is now. That, my friends, is a good thing!

My sex education consisted of a lesson about bees, flowers and pollination. No. I'm not joking — it was literally a book on birds and bees. I went to a Catholic school. There was zero human element to my sex education at all. We also received a book about menstruation. (I don't even think they referred to it as a period then.) That was extent of my sex ed.

Oh, what I wouldn't give to have that book now — just to compare it with the stuff that's available today. I was recently flipping through my son's Life Science book. There is a ton of information on the human reproductive system. It's all laid out for them. I did not have that when I was a kid. We talked about reproduction in terms of plants and animals. Not humans. The human part came along years later in high school when we got to health class.

Our parents did their best to prepare us for sex, but it was nothing like the conversations we're having with our children now. I clearly remember my mother stepping widely around this issue by saying something like, "It happens between a man and a woman when you're in love and married." It was at this point that a reference to God was mentioned to make sure the point was clear. I took her encouragement to mean: Do not have sex until you are married. I'm pretty sure most of my friends had a similar conversation with their mothers.

When we had our special talk, my mother was clearly nervous, and it was completely awkward, uncomfortable and not really a two-way discussion. We were in her bedroom laying on the bed looking at the ceiling. Now, as a mother, I am fully aware that the delicate conversations are hard to have while looking point blank in your child's face, however, some of these conversations require dialogue. This wasn't that time. This talk was more matter of fact. No room for discussion, or questions. That was it. The conversation was finished. Quite frankly, I probably wouldn't have asked questions if I had them. I'm pretty sure I ran out of her room when it was over.

Yet, on a much more exciting note, my mother would add her own flair to the situation when she had an audience. She would save these dittys for use on special occasions. When I would be getting ready with my girlfriends to go to the school dances she would say, to all of us, much to my embarrassment, "When you're dancing with a boy, leave room for the holy ghost and absolutely no TT. What is TT, you ask? That would be for Titty Touching for those of you who did not have the pleasure of enduring my mother during adolescence. Then she walked out of the room. End of story. Although I was mortified, my friends and I laughed about that one the rest of the night.

But really, what did I know? I was a tweenage girl, who went to Catholic church every Sunday. I knew boys were cute. I knew my curiosity was starting to pique. I knew there were games like Spin the Bottle and Truth or Dare that kids were too afraid to play the way they really wanted to. There was a lot of truth and not a lot of dare happening.

Speaking of curiosity, I have a hilarious story to share. I knew there were rated R movies with nudity on HBO, I just didn't understand what the fuss was all about. One night I attempted to sneak into the TV room late, while everyone was asleep, to see if I could find a "bad" movie. I just had to find out what made them so bad. I crept slowly toward the tv, wondering what the heck I might see. I was a little terrified, and a lot excited. I sat silently on the couch, grabbed the remote, and clicked the tv on. I turned down the volume as quickly as I could so no one would hear me. I was just about to the right channel to get my reward, when I got spooked by a noise. Shit! I thought someone was coming. I switched off the TV, praying that I didn't get caught, and scurried back to my room in a sweat. I never tried it again. Such a chicken. I have no idea what I was hoping to see. Naked people? The act of sex? Who knows. All I did know was that I had male friends who were checking out their father's stash of Playboy magazines, and at 12 years old they were most definitely not reading the articles. I just had to find out more.

When those hormones kick in so does the confusion, curiosity, embarrassment. When I was a child these very natural feelings weren't acknowledged in the same way they are today. No one said to us, "Hey, I get it. I've been there. I know you're going through a major change in your chemical makeup. Here's how we can work through it." Now that things are different, I've been having conversations with friends and clients for years about this particular stage in our kid's lives. Today's sex education is way more invasive than my barely sex talk was. Questions, books, videos, support groups, nothing is off limits. It's all planned in. You even know well in advance what year they will start talking about it in school.

When it comes to the sex stuff, it's not a comfy conversation for any of us, adults or parents. My opinion: The best way to tackle The Sex Talk is head on. If you have a lot of open communication in your family from the get go, it has the potential to be less awkward when you have to deal with more delicate issues. But regardless, it's still not the most fun conversation you'll ever have with your parents, or kids.

Here's the way I deal with the sex talk with my kids. I'm honest and educational. I use anatomically correct language. I talk about emotions and responsibility, especially in today's climate around sexuality and the #metoo movement. I share some vulnerability about what it's like from both sides. As with all conversations with kids, I want to be relatable. If you tell a story about your experiences (no matter the subject), you're showing your kids that you're human too. That's the magic. Being open and honest allows both you and them to navigate this space without shame, and allows space for them to communicate back with you when there are questions. I mean, who do you want your kids to go to for answers? You? Or the Interwebs?

Exactly. You got this. Good luck. Lemme know how it goes! My contact info is in the back of the book.

## BECAUSE... *Teenage Dating Firsts!*

It's one thing to have a crush. It's a different thing to actually go through with expressing your feelings for another person or vice versa and have it turn into something, right? I can remember when the shift happened for me in every one of my relationships. That moment when it goes from flirty friends to a bona fide couple. Each and every time this happened for me, it was equally nerve wracking. But that very first boyfriend was especially scary and intimidating.

When you make the decision to take your relationship to the next level my friends, you've officially entered the realm of dating. Gulp! I mean, do you remember what it was like to be as a dating teenager? All of those firsts?! Oy, those were some crazy times. The butterflies, the emotions, the questions — so many different feelings going on at once, you felt like you could literally explode!

There were a lot of "What If's" that came up when I was a young teenager about to enter the dating pool. Questions around worthiness and acceptance. Am I good enough to go out with this person? What about that person? Will my friends judge me for going out with this person? For me, there was nothing like the insecurities that came with dating for the first time.

Dating is tricky no matter what age you're experiencing it. I had these ideals built in my head around how romantic relationships are supposed to be. Many thanks to all the rom-coms out there. I set the expectation that I was going to be swept off my feet by Prince Charming and have a fairy tale experience. It wasn't all lollipops and rainbows, fancy dates and no arguments.

What I actually got was very different. Not that it was bad, it was just real life. A lot of it was fun, going to the movies or hanging out with friends, waterskiing and ATV riding in the mud. Some of it wasn't fun. Teenage jealousy and insecurity lead to fights about things like me wanting to spend time with my friends. This made my boyfriend feel left out. I didn't know how to deal with the hard stuff, especially as a teenager.

I didn't know how to do it the right way. By "do it" I mean facilitate a respectful, communicative, loving relationship with my partner. I was a teenager! I could barely brush my teeth without being reminded. How was I supposed to be cultivating mature adult relationships? Come to find out, like everything else, It's all through trial and error. Well, I was getting the error part right.

On top of the emotional roller coaster that is adolescent dating, I realized I was now embarking on my first foray into intimacy with another person. I experienced a lot of "firsts" which is totally awkward, intimidating, and potentially a little embarrassing. The excitement of a new relationship beginning, learning about one another, being nervous about doing and saying the wrong things, trying to impress each other, the first kiss with a new partner — it's all so sweet and exciting.

Speaking of first kisses, there's something to be said for intimate exploration when you're dating. I mean, who even knew how to kiss properly that first time? Playing tug of war with someone else's tongue is very different than practicing on your pillow in bed at night (You know you did that, so don't try to deny it.)

I remember my first real kiss. I was beyond nervous. Oddly, there were all kinds of questions going through my mind like, "What is this going to feel like?" "Am I going to be grossed out?" "How long does a real kiss last?" "What if he uses his tongue?" I'm not sure how I appeared on the outside, but on the inside, I was freaking out.

The only experience I had up to this point were my pillow and a few pecks on the lips I had received playing truth or dare. My heart was beating so hard I thought it would beat out of my chest! We were in his car. Classic, right? He drove me home from youth group. This was the first time he drove me home when no one else was in the car. It felt so grown up! He pulled into my driveway. I said, "Goodnight," and was about to get out of the car, but I could tell something was about to happen, so I lingered for a moment. He smiled at me, and slowly leaned in and kissed me.

It's a miracle I didn't throw up on our shoes. But in fact, I survived. And like so many other stories you hear, it wasn't a take your breath away, make you wanna be lip locked forever kind of kiss. It was wet, sloppy and quick. He looked at me to make sure it was okay. I remember feeling awkward afterward, and yet and somehow, I was not deterred. It was messy, but I liked it! I went back for more because it was exhilarating and new. Clearly it got better as we got to know one another. First kisses turned into make out sessions in the backseat of that car, a 1985 Camaro. Good God, if that car could talk...

This is also when I start to learn how to be a couple. Bringing together your time, ways and beliefs — understanding them and respecting them. Creating a relationship on a more intimate level than the physical takes a lot of work and commitment.

So often, especially when we're so young, we have a tendency to put our partners on pedestals. We think the sun rises and the moon sets on them and we silently expect them to believe the same about us. While that's all very romantic and wonderful, it's setting us up for a difficult road because it's unrealistic. We don't anticipate the adolescent jealousy and immaturity that plays a part in the equation.

Learning how to be open and vulnerable with another human being can be difficult. It can be intimidating and uncomfortable to share raw unfiltered feelings with your partner, especially in the beginning of your relationship. Communication and respect are two of the 5 Essentials. These are either gonna make, or break the relationship. This is where I started to learn how to work through these.

Being able to voice my desires for the first time, in a way that was not demanding or felt needy was super important. I wanted my partner to see me as an independent, strong person who could articulate my feelings no matter what the situation. When I started dating for the first time, I muddled through it the best way I could. Sometimes it was with grace, and other times it wasn't. Being completely exposed with your partner took some getting used to. For me it was something I wasn't completely comfortable with until much later in my life. It wasn't easy opening up my heart to someone else without having an element of fear associated with it.

Because I was a serial relationship haver from the beginning, I didn't get to experience a lot of first date jitters, I dove right in every time. Snagged them and didn't let them go until the relationship was no longer serving either one of us. I look back on my romantic relationships with a lot of love and gratitude. Each of them served a different purpose and taught me about myself on greater levels. I appreciate the time I spent with each of my former boyfriends.

## BECAUSE... *Sowing Oats!*

You guys, do you remember the block of time in your life when you were footloose and fancy free? Did you ever have that? I did, and it was pretty freaking amazing. This was end of high school through college pretty much. Those were the years when I really threw caution to the wind and allowed myself to explore, experiment and learn about myself and my power to choose my path. This was the time in my life when I really began to understand why my relationships were important. They're the years where I learned so much about myself and about the people I chose to have in my life. These are the years where I created my core group of friends. This was the time in my life where my true life-long friendships and relationships were formed.

After I went through a terrible break up, I spent some time without a boyfriend. I wanted to end high school and go to college unattached. It was a good decision. Those few years were some of my best memory-making years. I hung out with a lot of friends. I went to parties I hadn't attended before because I had a boyfriend who was older. He didn't like to go to high school parties. So, we didn't. Finally, I got to know people I hadn't had the opportunity to during school. It was a really great growing time.

I highly recommend having a time in your life to sow your oats, as they say. This can happen at a different time for all of us. For me, this time was about finding out where I had been missing out on life. Because I had always had a boyfriend when my friends were going to parties, I was going on dates and missing out on the bigger gatherings with my squad (as the young people call it today.) I was a teenager. While FOMO is a term we're all familiar with now, it existed back then too, and I had it. I needed to know what I was missing out on. Where were the parties? Who was going? What was happening at said parties?!?

Some of my sowing oats stories I will take to the grave with me, others bring me back to places that make me laugh out loud. In high school, I remember spending hours getting ready to go to parties with my girlfriends. We traded outfits and scrunched our hair with blow dryer diffusers and Aussie Sprunch Spray until it was so big we could barely fit through the door (or so it seemed).

There was always an empty house where parents were away. We took advantage whenever we could. We would gather our friends together and party like it was 1999. We may or may not have even played that song at the party! We slurped Jell-O shots, drank "hunch punch" (a boozy concoction that basically consisted of every kind of alcohol mixed together with fruit punch), and danced on the furniture to *Friends In Low Places* by Garth Brooks. Hey, no judgement. It was the late 80's.

At one of those epic parties, I was on a couch engaged in a make out session with a boy that I liked at the time. This guy also happened to be the middle school principal's son. Only to have that same party crashed by said dad/principal hours later...I mean, you wanna talk about being embarrassed? I never lived that one down!

In college my adventures continued with friends I would make in my new city. We quickly created a routine that was not for the faint of heart. There were rarely nights we were home! Frat parties, dance clubs and nickel beer nights were on the agenda. My squad was down for all of it.

I mean there was the one time we were having a party in our apartment. You know the kind. Underage drinking, a ton of people, loud music, and random debauchery happening in dark corners. Inevitably, the cops were called (thanks neighbors). I have no idea how many people were at the party, but I'm pretty sure we were exceeding the maximum for fire safety. Needless to say, once the very attractive police officers showed up we turned it down, but not for long because they decided to stay for a bit. They even came back the next day to check on us. Aww...isn't that sweet?

You guys, I'm sharing these stories because I want you to know how important it is to have a time in your life for yourself. A time to sow your oats without care. It's thanks to those years that I don't feel like I missed out on anything. I learned how to truly appreciate living during those years, and carried it through for the rest of my life. My moments of care free life have made me a better mom, and most certainly a better partner. I have no regrets! I've lived. If you have memories like this, cherish them. If you have kids, let them have their experiences.

I want my kids to explore the world. I want them to have a time in their lives when they're sowing their oats and creating their *Friends In Low Places* memories. I want them to have stories about the time they got caught making out with the principal's kid at a party by the actual principal who crashed the party. I want them to build friendships that will last a lifetime because those years did that for me.

I'm sure that when my kids get to that age, I'll be sitting up, a wreck, waiting for the door to open, letting me know they're home. Or checking their text messages and tracking devices. I won't be prying into their stories. If they want to share them with me, great, but I won't be forcing it out of them. We all need stories to take to the grave — regardless if it's for a friend or one of our own.

The time I truly had to myself created some of my greatest memories and greatest friendship relationships. Those years allowed me to come into my own and grow up. To learn to take responsibility for myself and my actions, positive or negative. To find my voice and learn how to use it. That was a gift. Having that time, unbeknownst to me at the time, better prepared me for my future.

## BECAUSE... *Passion!*

The word passion wears two hats for me. There is the intense hot version which leaves you breathless. This is the short-term version. Then there is the slower burn, that creates intensity over a longer period of time. Each has a deep meaning, and specific place in my life.

There are specific instances in our lives where we are swept off of our feet. It's unexpected. Intense. I use the word Passionate. Romantic relationships can't survive without at least some of this chemistry. I have a passionate connection with my husband, but we didn't meet until later so for context, in this section of the book, I didn't know him.

I have a few significant memories in the vault that have come to the surface during the writing of this part of this book that are each very different. The first was a sweep-me-off-my-feet makeout session. The second, a long-term relationship. How did passion get me to each of these situations? Let's talk about it.

The first time I was left breathless with passion was the night of my graduation from high school. It was completely unexpected. If you live in a small town everyone knows everyone — or they know someone who knows everyone. That's what it was like in Palm Coast, Florida in the 80's and early 90's.

The night I graduated from high school, we went to a friend's house. His parents weren't home. With our closest hundred or two hundred friends we had a party. At one point in the evening,

I found myself talking to an older guy. He had been around for a while, we had just never met before that night. We ended up having an intelligent conversation about college and life. That was it.

When it was time to go, my bestie and I said goodbye to our friends and headed to her car. I was the designated driver for the evening so I was completely sober. Because we lived in Florida it was hot out, so we immediately rolled down the windows to wave to our friends. Before I could start the car, Mr. Mysterious appeared at my window. Without saying one word, he looked into my eyes, took me face in his hands, leaned in and kissed me like we were the last two people on earth. It was so freaking romantic. It went on for a good minute or so. I was left breathless. My friend sat there in shock, watching, from the passenger seat. After that, he let me go, said goodbye, and walked away into the night. It took me a few minutes to gather myself up after that encounter. Needless to say, he made quite the impression with that goodbye.

Ridiculously, we would not come into contact again until a few years later, after college. He showed up at my parent's house unannounced to ask me out to dinner. We definitely had a chemistry that would weave in and out of our lives for a little while until we eventually lost touch.

Don't you love stories like that? Classic chick flick, girl meets boy, passionate moment and then nothing ever comes of it. I think everyone should have an experience like that. One that leaves them wondering what could've been. It's romantic.

Then there's the other kind of chemistry. The kind of slower passion that leads to a long-term relationship. My college boyfriend and I had that kind of undeniable chemistry. To the point where it was ridiculous. We couldn't keep our hands off of each other.

Our chemistry was multiplied because my man and I were both in college in different states, we didn't get to spend a lot of time together other than the occasional long weekend, school breaks and summer vacations for 2 years. That relationship was nurtured over the phone (no email back then), we got to know each other during our hour's long conversations and snail mail letters. The time we spent apart only heightened our desire to be together. We learned to appreciate one another through distance, cultivating our own communication style that worked for us at the time.

When we had time together we were basically tangled up in each other. Literally. It was insanity, and the best thing, all at the same time. That kind of passion should be bottled and sold in mass quantities. That kind of attraction is why babies are born. We could not take our hands off of each other when we were together. And it wasn't just physical — we really enjoyed each other's company. We were social with friends, we traveled, we loved to go dancing. It was a great time. It just wasn't great timing.

Physical connections are funny things. They make us hungry for more. They teach us the value of intimacy and passion. The glory of being appreciated and acknowledged at our absolute most vulnerable. They're raw and primal and quite necessary in a romantic relationship.

Ideally your passions should make you feel strong, feisty and powerful. I caution you never to take it for granted.

Nurture your passion, feed it and keep it alive. Even after what seems like a hundred years have passed, and your kids have sucked the life out of you, and have left the house. ESPECIALLY then. Make your physical relationship a focus. Connect on all the levels. It takes a lot of work to keep the passion in a relationship, but it's worth every bit of it. And let's be honest, when you're in a loving partnership, there's nothing like a good romp in the hay!

## BECAUSE... *Living Together!*

Be ready for it. It seems like such a romantic idea when you are dating. Sleeping over at someone else's house and having a toothbrush there is VERY different than actual cohabitation. Living together is about taking the next step. And by the way, don't get rid of your own place, unless you are really ready to be with someone ALL. THE. TIME. Depending on how ready you are to do it — the moving in with your partner can take things to the next level, or the last level. Like I said, you've got to really be ready.

I've lived in "sin" exactly two times in my life. I married one of them. The other, well, it didn't last. Living together takes a relationship to a whole new level and for me, it was either make it or break it. This momentous act has the potential to change the trajectory of a relationship simply by exposing quirks and shortcomings.

These things like leaving the toilet seat up or putting dirty clothes on the floor NEXT to the hamper (I mean, this one will follow me for my entire existence). They may seem like small nuances, but they build up. Rather than bottling up the angry feelings because you're feeling like your partner isn't carrying their part of the load, you should nip that in the bud early on. Have the conversation. You know me. I'm all about that open communication.

No doubt it's exciting when you first move in with your partner. Especially if it's in a new place for both of you. It's definitely harder to move in with someone where they've already established residency. When it's fresh and new for both of you, the playing field is level, so to speak.

I remember when I moved in with my boyfriend. Our parents gave us some furniture from their respective houses, and we combined stuff that we had from our prior places that we had shared with roommates. We started playing house. Except along with playing house comes responsibility. Sure, it's fun to have friends over for dinner parties, sleep naked in your own home and put your feet on the furniture. It's not fun to clean, maintain all the shit and decide who is going to do what when it comes right down to it.

If you are new to it, living together takes work on more levels than you're likely used to, so before you make the commitment to it, be prepared. I wrote this chapter to have this exact discussion with you. A discussion I wish that someone would have had with me.

Cohabitation is not a sleepover, it's a long-term undertaking. You really get to know someone when you spend most of your time together under one roof. And sometimes you find out that it just doesn't work. In my case of the first guy I lived with, it was a contributor to the demise of that particular relationship.

I had a job that required me to travel 90% of the time. I was super young and loved the adventure. Because I was gone all week, he started developing his own social life. We didn't spend any time connecting. In the end, our issues were bigger than who was or wasn't doing what in the house. What was actually happening is that we were leading two completely different lives during the week and hanging out on the weekends. We weren't really talking, and communication on important issues was fairly non-existent.

Because of all of that, the space between kept growing wider. We ended up more like roommates than romantic partners.

And, as per my opening statement, we just weren't ready. That relationship didn't last long after we moved in together. I wasn't ready to be a "housewife." Somehow, I became responsible for doing all of the grocery shopping, laundry and dinner making while holding down a full-time job at the age of 23. I also realized through this relationship that I needed more than small town Florida living. Since my day job had me traveling, I had caught the bug and wanted to see more.

I learned a lot in the short time I lived with someone other than my husband. I learned that I wasn't willing to compromise my bigger desires, especially at such a young age. I learned that I could stand on my own and support myself. I learned that I wasn't ready to commit to the "whole package" of marriage at that point. I realized I needed to do more exploring in the world.

If you're considering taking the leap with your main person — do some serious talking about expectations, the ones you have for yourself and the ones you have with your partner. Decide beforehand who's paying for what — that may seem silly, but it can be a relationship breaker! And most of all, communicate!!

# BECAUSE... *Breaking Up Is A Process!*

Just as important as how you got together, the process of breaking up needs some time and nurturing to work through. Most of us try really hard to short circuit the process of ending a relationship. In so many ways. We don't want to feel the feelings of loss. We're going to talk about *not* doing that in this section.

Relationships don't always go well. You won't always be on the same page as your partner. If that lasts long enough, and you have exhausted all possibilities of being together, sometimes the best thing to do is to end it. If that's the case, allow yourself some time to heal. That's the most important part, the healing.

Breaking up with someone is never easy, even when you know it's the right thing to do, faking that you're okay isn't helping. Be honest with your feelings and give yourself the proper space you need to recover before you go out looking for a new one. And the thing is, there's no approved recovery time period. It could be as short as a few weeks or as long as a few years. It all depends on how you treat yourself during the process.

Sometimes you have no idea why a break up happened, and other times the message was loud and clear. I had one boyfriend in particular that I was blindsided by when it came to our break up. We had been together for a couple of years and one day I got a note from him hand delivered by his cousin, who also happened to be one of my best friends. She gave the shitty document to me in the car on our way to school. A freaking note. It's like the equivalent of a breakup via text these days. We had been together for almost two years, our families were friends, and I got a note. No phone call, no showing up at my door to break it off. A NOTE!!! I was devastated. I felt like my heart had stopped.

All I can remember the note saying was, "You're too good for me," or something ridiculous like that. Of course, to add insult to injury, this terrible note arrived right before the big home-coming dance where I just happened to be in the running for homecoming queen. Who does that? The kicker was that there was absolutely nothing wrong in our relationship — or so I thought. We rarely fought, we had a great time together, our families loved each other. He and I had zero contact after that note. Like none. That breakup really did knock me off kilter. So much so that I shut that side of me down. I was unwilling to expose my heart on that level again for a long time.

The thing that sticks out for me when it comes to break ups are the range of feelings I went through. The tears, emotions, guilt...all the things. I blamed myself. I blamed him. It wasn't until I was older and could discuss it with my girlfriends that I realized it truly is a loss. That kind of loss requires grieving. I wanted to breeze over it. I did not want to feel the separation feelings. For a little while, I was ugly-crying in bed, feeling sorry for myself, eating pints of Ben and Jerry's, while binge watching bad TV. I didn't want to talk to anyone about it, I wanted to forget it. I didn't know how to allow myself to go through all of the emotions so I could properly heal. I definitely wanted to bypass it.

After that very short phase, I spent some time going out and partying it up until I was so exhausted I couldn't see straight. I sowed those oats again! I wanted to focus on other things to the extreme after that break up. I really tried to avoid it rather than work through it. Granted I was seventeen and looking for a distraction. So, I chose to dive head first into work, spending time with my friends and booking up my schedule so I didn't have to be alone for too long.

Here's my best breakup advice: Allow yourself the time to grieve. If not, you take those wounds into your next relationship, and the one after that. Heal. Get comfortable being with yourself. Ask yourself what you learned from that relationship. What will you do differently in the next one? You have to eventually put yourself back out there if you're someone who wants to spend your life with a partner romantically. If you work through your heartbreak, instead of ignoring it, you can look forward to new romantic opportunities in the future. Give yourself a fresh start. Then when you've found your happy, go find someone to share it with.

We really do learn so much about ourselves through our relationships. How to grow and nurture them, and how not to handle them. A lot of it is through trial and error and all of it is through effort. Different phases of our lives create different relationships, ultimately teaching us how to appreciate all of them. As you reminisce on your early relationships, refer back to the 5 Essentials to see if you were using any of them as you cultivated your relationships. Use them as a tool moving forward with your loved ones so you can create long lasting, fulfilling relationships as you continue to grow.

*Woo Hoo!! You've made it through the relationship foibles of adolescence and young adulthood. I hope some of my embarrassing took you to a place that made you smile at your memories, and maybe learn some about yourself and your relationships along the way. You see? We all have our shit. Hopefully we all make it out the other side having learned a lot about ourselves in the process, with only some minor scrapes and bruises.*

## BECAUSE...

# The One!

The One. THE One. The other person on the planet that you have decided to create a life with. And man alive, that is no small feat. This is the One that, after your relationship with yourself, matters the most. This is the One that has the potential to go the distance. It will be one of your greatest accomplishments. It will be one of the hardest relationships you've ever had and sustained. It will take work, compromise and more love than you thought you had available to you. You will have battle scars and doubts along the way, but in the end, it will be completely worth it.

I know all of this because I have it. It's the one relationship that I will make a priority until my last breath. As of this writing, I've been with Will for a total of 21 years — married for 17 of them. I can unequivocally say that while we've had our share of not so easy times, there's no one I would rather do this life with than him.

Let me preface this by saying I'm extremely aware that I am not the norm in the realm of long- term relationships these days. I think that's sad, because a lot of people throw in the towel too early. Today, it's easier to walk away than it is to put in the work. But in certain situations, I get it. I got lucky when I met my husband.

I do want to share some of my experience with you. After years of being a coach, doing my own work, and helping others in this way, I've noticed some things that come up again and again that lead to a more connected and long-term-abled relationship. If that seems like it's for you, the person you choose to go the distance with has to be a few things for you and vice versa to make that long-term work well. To begin with you both have to do the work. You can't sustain a long-term relationship that's one sided. You both have to be willing to get uncomfortable and be honest about what's going on for you. You read above about communicating, and the importance of listening and being honest.

Next you have to have a clear understanding of those 5 Essentials. Like I've talked about in the intro of this book, respect, trust, support, intimacy and communication absolutely, and of course apply to the One love of your life. When it comes to the Essentials and associating it with the person you've chosen to spend the rest of your life with, these are the things you focus on every day.

Finally, you have to be able to laugh at yourself and each other. Don't take everything so seriously. Have fun together. And for god's sake, like one another. Forever is a long time to settle.

So many women have to kiss a lot of frogs to figure out they deserve a prince. My list of frogs wasn't very long. So, how did I know when I had met my "one love?" Keep reading, I'll share my story.

## BECAUSE... *Finding The One!*

Once upon a time, a girl walked into a bar....

And her entire life changed behind layers of a colorful drink and hip bar lighting.

I mean, isn't that how your future husband caught your eye? With a sparkling smile and quick wit? Well that's what happened to me. He'll tell you that he heard me laugh as I was walking into the bar and was attracted to me before he laid eyes on me. I'm not sure I believe that, but the romantic in me loves it.

Our meeting was definitely unexpected and a little complicated, which can sometimes happen when you meet the person you'll eventually spend the rest of your life with. When I met Will, I was in a long term, serious relationship. Like I was telling you in last section about relationships growing up, the relationship I was in when I met Will was really disconnected at the time. We were kinda just going through the motions and were drifting apart.

While I certainly wasn't looking for a romantic relationship so soon after a breakup, it was clear that I had feelings for the new guy that I had extended beyond a platonic friendship. So I did what any crazy twenty four year old woman would do. In October 1997, I packed my bags (and my car), left my dog with my parents, and drove a thousand miles from Florida to New York City to be with my One. That was 21 years ago. I had found my home with Will, and I never left.

I realize not everyone finds the love of their life the way I found mine. We found each other unexpectedly, and quite randomly. I know for a lot of you it took work and determination. I think people feel pressure when we hit a certain age to create the spouse and babies. Most of the time life rarely happens the way we plan it will. I certainly didn't plan to meet Will.

I have friends who met their One when they were kids and are still happily together. I have other friends who are on their second go round because their first One wasn't their forever One. Here's the thing when it comes to this specific relationship: you can't settle for anything less than what you truly desire to experience. Anything less will be unsatisfying. You have to believe your person is out there no matter what stage of life you're in. Sometimes the One comes into your life early, and other times they come in later than you anticipated. It's divine timing. You have to be open, trusting and patient. If you want it, your One is out there.

## BECAUSE... *Being With The One!*

Before you take the leap into a deeper relationship with your One, you should be clear on what you want in your person. After my prior relationship ended, I took a break. I took some time to myself to really think about what I wanted in a partner. In a complete partnership. I wanted to be able to speak my mind. I wanted to be challenged intellectually. I wanted to be sexually compatible. I wanted someone who respected my opinion and encouraged my Joie de Vivre. I wanted someone who looked passed the face and body and saw the heart and soul. I didn't put any significance on looks or ambition. I didn't care about "the stuff" he had or the job he did.

Turns out, a random long haired, multiple pierced bartender in New York City would end up being the smartest, kindest, most supportive and loving person I have ever known. Not exactly the type I had been with before, but the universe had something else in store for me and I was totally on board. We just gelled from the beginning.

It's hard to explain, there was, and still is, something about him that made me want to be around him. The way he viewed the world, the way he was considerate of our relationship, his thoughtfulness. Before I moved back to New York, we would talk on the phone for hours — back when you actually had to pay for long distance service — and rack up hundreds of dollars in phone bills. After I moved to NY (and in with him in a tiny postage stamp sized apartment), we would take long walks around the city, exploring new neighborhoods and enjoy being in the moment. We didn't plan our life, we just let it happen. No pressure, no timeline. It didn't take long for me to realize that THIS guy was the one I couldn't live without.

When we decided to embark on our adventure together we would spend hours talking about the ins and outs of relationships. We would have deep, intellectual conversations about social issues and world events. We had a lot of sex. We figured each other out by being inquisitive and really listening to one another. We bought books of questions and would ask each other for our opinions. We weren't afraid to disagree — respectfully. And this is important people. You've got to be able to argue without hurting each other.

If you learn anything in this chapter it should be this: RESPECT your partner. And make sure they respect you back. No matter what. Even when you disagree. Will and I made a pact at the beginning of our relationship that we would never disrespect one another by using derogatory words toward each other. Now, I realize that can be difficult. It's easy to throw a word out because you're frustrated or mad, but calling your partner a name is not nice. Words hurt — a lesson we all learn throughout our lives. So why would you be okay with the one person who's supposed to be your biggest supporter and encourager saying unkind or nasty things to you? In all the years we've been together, neither one of us has ever called the other a negative word. (Maybe in our heads we have, but never out loud.) That matters.

Do I always agree with him? No.

Does he probably want to kill me sometimes? I'm sure.

Do we question some of our decisions? Of course.

But we have found a way to communicate that works for us. We don't scream at one another or fly off the handle. We talk. We digest information. We act like adults and work on a situation together. That's probably one of the secrets to our success. Because of that, I can honestly say we rarely disagree or argue. And maybe because we've been together so long, we just know how the other person ticks, but we really do respect one another.

Respect isn't the only thing you need for your One recipe. Like I've been talking about throughout this book, there are a lot of elements in relationships. The difference in the One is that you've chosen to be with this one person in every way. Stripped down to the core. This is the relationship where you'll share things that no one else knows about you. This is the one that you will commit to working on even when the going gets so tough it might seem hard to see the light at the end of the tunnel. The trick to this specific relationship, the one that you've committed to for the long haul, is that you have to be each other's first priority, even after the kids show up in your world and will need a good deal of your time.

Yep, I said it. Make one another your first priority. It makes you better at everything you do. Including your parenting.

Please don't let your relationship fall by the wayside. It takes work, every day. I learned this from my parents who were married for 47 years. Ever since we were young, My mom would tell us that my dad would always be her first priority — because let's face it, one day my brother and I wouldn't live with them anymore. We would be off building our own lives. And because of that, that's exactly what my parents did. They prioritized their relationship, they were number one in each other's eyes. Life wasn't always easy for them, but they managed through it as a team and truly loved each other through it all. They set the bar high for us in terms of marriage and family and for that I will always be grateful.

## BECAUSE... *Keeping The One!*

There will be times in your relationship when you're not feeling in line with your partner. When you're in a rut. That's what I like to call it. A space where you may not be firing on all cylinders or you're miscommunicating. When that's happening, you have to be wise enough to take a step back and focus.

My marriage is not immune to the rut. We go through it the same way everyone else does. We get so caught up in our own jobs, kids, and other things that we lose focus on one another because we think we're solid. Sometimes months go by and we haven't had a date or any real alone time that wasn't mired by exhaustion. That's when the mind can play terrible tricks on me. I start to wonder if my partner is losing interest. I create all these crazy ideas in my head that are the furthest thing from reality. I work myself into a tizzy. I've done it — especially after our kids were born. Talk about an adjustment!

Will and I don't shoot for perfection (dumb word) we strive for connecting as much as we can. But once he or I speaks up and says something like, "I need more attention because i feel like we're drifting apart." Or I send a funny email with the subject line that says, "Um, it's been 2 weeks since I've seen you naked...that's a problem." You bet our issue will be addressed. We have fun with it instead of pointing fingers when we hit that rut. We've all been there. It's all good. Pay attention and give your relationship the time it deserves.

I coach a lot of clients on how to manage their way through their relationship issues. The biggest mistake we can make is taking one another for granted. It is easy to assume everything is fine. Many of us fall into a mindless groove as we go about our days. Get up, get the kids ready, send them to school, go to work, come home, do whatever we need in the evening (some kid related activity probably), have dinner, yell through the bedtime routine (you know who you are), watch TV and go to bed. Day in and day out for eighteen years (or longer.) All of this activity but no connection. Just people bumping into one another at the beginning and end of their days. Some of us survive that — most of us will not. This behavior in the long-term makes us wonder if that is all there is. A day full of disconnected activity? It's boring.

There is so much more available to you and your families than that. That long-term disconnection is not what any relationship should be. Connection IS the purpose. Sometimes it takes a while to get out of the rut because you've been in it for so long and other times, it's easy to snap out of. The trick to ending a rut is making the choice. The continued and ongoing choice of prioritizing your partnership.

For Will and me, it's about those tiny moments we make for each other during the day. We schedule time alone for date night, or a chat around the breakfast table after we've excused the kids on a Sunday morning. He and I try hard to be aware of one another's needs, and make each other feel special. It's okay to say no to your children in favor of your partner. Yes. I said it. That shows them that you value your partnership. Keep your interests piqued with each other, because years from now, when the kids are off having their own adventures, you want to start having new ones yourselves. Prioritizing one another is the best thing you can do for your union.

Have the sex — even when you don't want to. Even when you're so exhausted and have seven hundred million other things on your mind — do it. It doesn't have to be all fancy and passionate and last for hours. Does that even happen in real life anyway? Sometimes it's five minutes in the closet because the kids are home and you don't want to get caught. Figure out a way to make intimacy a regular thing. And by regular, I mean as often as you can.

There will be times in your relationship when you're having less sex than usual (ahem, kids) and there will be times when it's like you first started dating (ahem, vacation without the kids). Whatever it is that keeps you both happy in that department — keep doing it. Plus, it's fun and even when you don't want to and you end up all breathless and sweaty, you'll wonder why you don't do that more often. Ya with me? Good. Enjoy!

Forgive each other. Frequently, and often. I can't tell you how many people I work with, and know in real life, who are grudge holders. It's terrible for so many reasons. Not having the capacity to forgive and move on is something that will not only hurt your relationship, it can cripple you personally with stress. Have you heard the St. Augustine quote, "Resentment is like drinking poison and waiting for the other person to die." This is absolutely true. It's only harming you.

Life is too short to go through it mad or dissatisfied with someone you love. Yes, we all have our not so great moments. Why? Because none of us is perfect. That means everyone you know is just like you, and makes mistakes. Be a forgiver. There are a lot of things in life we can't control, but we can control our feelings toward the people we love. Forgive your partner after you've had a disagreement. (and apologize while you're at it, because I'm sure you're at fault too.) Then move on. Situation over, put it to bed.

And do your relationship a real favor. Actually, let it go. Don't bring it back up at a later time when you're not in a good place. No one wants baggage held over their head. This stuff is hard enough, mistakes don't require reminding. We are all human and self-deprecating enough that we don't need any outside reminders of our flaws. Forgiveness may not always be easy, depending on the issue, but if you really are in it for the long haul, then you're going to have to find it in your heart to be a forgiving person.

Instead of resentment. Try appreciation. Especially when it's difficult. Appreciate one another and accept who your partner is. You cannot change someone into becoming who **you** want them to be. Do not for one-minute think you can change your person, because you can't. Believe me. I've tried. We accept our differences and appreciate one another's quirks.

My husband is a jeans, tee shirt and sneakers kind of guy. You should see his collection. Vintage. And not that freshly minted "vintage." This is the real stuff.

He's a creature of habit and takes forever to make a decision about everything. It once took him three weeks to decide on a color for bathroom towels. This was before he met me, but still. I am a hurricane. A title my aunt gave me years ago, because I'm a force to be reckoned with. I have a lot of energy for someone who doesn't drink caffeine! I like to get things done and make quick decisions. Will and I are total opposites when it comes to our personalities. But instead of his laid back, relaxed personality driving my type A personality crazy, I decided to embrace all the things he does differently than I would and accept his quirks. I decided to appreciate them. He collects all kinds of stuff. He's got piles of comic books and postcards all over the place. As long as we can find a home for everything, we're in good shape.

Have fun! Look, if you're planning on spending a long time with your significant other then you should really enjoy spending time with one another. Travel, learn about the things you like individually and make the effort to do those things together. This only works if this goes both ways. If I was only interested in Will's life, and not vice versa, we wouldn't still be together.

My husband is a motorcycle enthusiast. Am I? Not particularly, but that never stopped me from going to Bike Week every year in Daytona Beach to walk around and see the sights. And lemme tell ya, after spending days looking at motorcycles, women in full body paint, and men in leather chaps it kinda makes you want to jump right into the culture. It's fascinating! It also didn't stop me from getting on his Harley and taking day trips with him to see scenic country sides. Please have fun and make it a point to laugh together. Life is about enjoyment, and it's so much greater when you get to share that with someone.

You guys, there are so many facets to having a great, long term, forever relationship. And we're all human, no one is perfect. Certainly not Will and I. Don't compare your anything — life, relationship, parenting, job, social life — with anyone else's. None of us are the same. We all have different things to deal with and different priorities. So just focus on you, your life, and your priorities. Tune out the noise and tune into your needs and the needs of your partner. You will thank me for this if you're not already doing it!

Will and I have been together for almost half of our lives. Yes, seriously. We've been through it all. Literally. All the ups and downs to the in-betweens. From the pure joy of marriage and babies, to profound loss. Financial stability and instability, and at one point, losing all of my retirement due to corporate greed (Thanks Worldcom!). From family crap that was never worth the trouble, to terrorist attacks (we survived 9/11 in real life) that could have ruined us. We've questioned decisions and stood firm in opinions. We've parented and partied — sometimes at the same time (that's more me than him though.) We've really liked and disliked each other, but we've always loved one another. It's not perfect, but it's ours and with a lot of work, determination and belief in our relationship I hope it lasts for a very long time.

PS: The #WhyAmIYelling? Because...*Marriage*!! book is in the works.

*Finding someone to spend forever with is truly special. It means you accept one another for who you are as individuals and appreciate it. It means you find ways to communicate through the disagreements. It means while you love one another, you truly like being together. Committing to one person for a lifetime is a huge decision and I applaud you if you've done it and put in the work, because it's one of the hardest relationships you'll ever have. It's also one of the greatest. When you find your "one" and you hold them tight, anything is possible.*

## BECAUSE...

# Building a Family!

Sometimes, after you've decided to go the distance with someone the next step for you might be to take your partnership to the next level by creating a family of your own. Making the decision to become parents is a biggie, and should not be taken lightly. Those kids, well, they're a commitment on a whole different level. Way past having a long-term relationship. Having a family is THE Commitment. Raising a human being is scary, fun, tricky and exciting. Like every other relationship you have, it's hard and takes work.

Will and I thought we were prepared to have kids because we were kids once ourselves. We had our own experiences that we wanted to emulate in some ways, and in other ways not so much. We prepared (and I use that term loosely) for this stage by taking stock in our own past relationships with our loved ones, pulling out the lessons we wanted to use from them. It all sounded so easy-peasy and ideal. HAHAHAHAHAHA! Sike!! That's not how it works — at least not completely.

## BECAUSE... *Our Family Begins!*

It was March 18th, 2005. I was wrapped in a towel, dripping wet from the bath I had just taken. I was standing in front of my husband who was sitting in his chair, reading the news after dinner. I held out a stick, and I was shaking. He looked at me quizzically and took it. The word in the little window said "pregnant." Will stood up and wrapped his arms around me. At this point I said, "Now what are we gonna do?" In my head I was a teenager, about to break the news to my parents, not the married for 4 years, 32 year-old woman that I was. I didn't feel "ready" to be pregnant, let alone a mother. He looked at me and said, "What do you mean? We're gonna have a baby, and it's gonna be great!"

There is something you should know about me. I am a planner. Not only am I really good at it, I love the order that planning brings to my often chaotic world. I had a plan for marriage. I definitely had a plan for babies. Yet, as the years have progressed, I have come to realize that the Universe works in its own mysterious ways, my beautiful and well-laid plans were foiled again and again by the Universe. Having these particularly large events of marriage and babies happened before I thought I, or my plans, were ready for them.

What I have come to learn is that you're never ready for the big events of your life. I used to say, "It's not a good time to... (insert event here)," because I thought we didn't have enough money or a big enough apartment or whatever excuse I could drum up to push off the conversation. When in reality, I was probably just a little bit afraid. I thought I would be in my thirties when I got married — I was 28. I thought I would have a baby at 35 — I was 33. Not too far off from my original plan, but enough to elicit some unease.

We became parents for the first time in 2005 and again in 2012, we have 2 very active, happy, healthy boys. And while I still did not feel like I was ready to birth my children, (not because I didn't think I'd be a good mother), I just literally was not ready for the marathon of the physical stamina of pushing a child out of my hoo-ha. Of course, I really had no choice but to face my fear. I mean, they couldn't stay in there forever!

Once they were on the outside, we quickly realized that we are not raising children, rather we're raising human beings. We take our job as parents very seriously, but, not too seriously. Happy medium, right? My mother always said from as far back as I can remember, "You will never know the amount of love I have for you until you become a parent yourselves." It tastes like vinegar to say this, but she was a million percent right. Nothing can prepare you for that. NOTHING.

I absolutely hated being pregnant. Sorry preggo lovers, I don't get the appeal, no offense. I have no good reason why I didn't enjoy the process. It's not like I had any real issues during my pregnancy. The only thing I can tell you is that I'm a type A control freak. Thus, not having control over what was happening to me was terrible. I had the easiest pregnancies on the planet, no sickness, proper amount of weight gain, good health. I just didn't like it either time. Why would you love to gain all that weight, have all of the limitations on food and beverages and then have to deal with the actual labor? I LOVE my babies, but the pregnancies were a drag.

My first birth story is super relevant here because that was the day I stopped being scared of the "what if's" surrounding major life events. I started to embrace the idea that while I may never feel ready for something. There is a bigger reason why my experience was unfolding the way it was. I needed to not be ready at that time in my life to realize it's okay to not be ready. I had to learn to give up control. The planning had to end, and I had to learn how to be okay in the moment, no matter what was happening. In the end it will always be okay. If it's not, its not the end.

I was overdue by 4 days, and I felt like a house. I was actually starting to fear the delivery less than the fact that he might stay in there forever. It was in the middle of the night after Thanksgiving dinner when my water finally broke. At the time, we were living in a one-bedroom apartment and my parents were visiting from Florida, sleeping on the pull-out couch in the living room. They had spent the first few days of their visit hovering over me, pacing around, suggesting I go on long walks to get the labor started. They only had a finite amount of time to be with us before they had to go back. My mother was becoming a wreck because she wanted to have time with her grandson! She could care less about me, just give her that baby! Cut to 4 o'clock in the morning, and I will not let Will wake them up. I wanted to start my labor without fanfare. Just the two of us. We eventually headed to the hospital, courtesy of my uncle who dropped us off on his way back upstate at around 9am.

I delivered my first-born son, Wyatt, on my 33rd birthday. I know. Awful, right!? Some people think it's cute. I did not take it that well. My birthday is my favorite day of the year. I'm a big celebrator of birthdays. I love them. Even though I loved my son more than any other being on the planet, I didn't want to share my birthday with him. I eventually I got over it, and realized that it's a special bond that only he and I share. That's pretty cool.

My life changed the day he was born. It's unexplainable the love we have for our children. I remember within seconds of having him that I knew firmly that I would throw myself in front of a moving train for him. My love for him was so crazy. No amount of book reading, or story sharing can prepare you for the over-whelming feelings of love after you have a child. For the record, I read exactly 2 pregnancy/baby books. And they happened to be the funny kind. Not the clinical ones.

My husband was a rock star with my pregnancy — up until the point of us actually having the kids. He had rarely been around them, talk about not being ready, he had zero experience. But in true fashion, he stepped up to the plate and faced it with me head on. From the minute our boys were born, he jumped right in, helping with all the stuff. Making sure they had everything they needed, letting me get rest, feeding, diapering, all of it. He wasn't a sometimes babysitter dad. He was a full on partner dad. Not one complaint. Except the exhaustion. Get used to it. That never goes away. Wyatt is now 13, his little brother Elias is 6, and I think I can count on 2 hands the amount of times I've slept through the night since they've been alive. Good times.

I was recently at an event speaking to another woman and she was having these similar feelings. She wanted to start a family with her husband, but she said she's not ready for all of the reasons I experienced. She didn't feel ready. She told me she's in a happy marriage, but they want a bigger place. She told me she's old enough for her window of conception to be narrowing. She was afraid that they wouldn't be able to afford it. I shared with her that I felt the same way, and that one day I realized I didn't want to pause my life anymore. I wanted to experience motherhood more than I wanted to be afraid of it, or be in control of it. By the end of the evening, we were both crying after sharing our stories. I'm pretty sure she went home with a new perspective.

If you're at a point in your life where you're questioning your readiness for that next step, that's totally normal. But please don't delay something life changing because you're afraid of it. Because you think you need more money in the bank (don't we all?), or because you don't have the right house. Sometimes throwing caution to the wind brings the greatest joy to your life, and you'll never regret it. Now go have a baby! HAHAHAHAHA!!!

# BECAUSE... *The Kind of Parent I Want to Be!*

Kids have a way of making you become hyper aware of everything. I started to become so much more aware of the state of the world. You start to take stock in all of the surroundings. Is it appropriate? Is it safe? Is it healthy? So many questions to keep a kid safe! From day one I've felt like I was winging it. I often still feel that way!

When I was pregnant I wondered what kind of parent I was going to be. I started to watch and critique other parents. (Note: I was not judging other parents, because, hey, you have no idea what other people's situations are). I simply wondered if I would use their techniques, or perhaps adopt a method that might work better for my family. I considered the way I was raised, and if I wanted to carry on some of the ways I was parented.

Many of us do not parent the same way we were parented, for a lot of reasons. Could be you had a shitty childhood and you don't want to have any part in raising a child the way you were raised. Could be that you had strict parents and you felt like you were ruled with an iron fist. Could be that you had too lenient parents and you wanted more discipline. I was recently talking to a friend about this. We both agreed that society, technology and education play a much bigger part in parenting these days than in past generations. We need to be more aware of circumstances going on in the world. It would be almost impossible to parent the same way our parents did.

"With great power comes great responsibility," said Uncle Ben in Spiderman, and he's absolutely right. Before our kids were born,

Will and I made conscious decisions and had honest discussions about what attributes we wanted to impart on our kids. Of course, the obvious, kindness, consideration, lovingness and compassion are all important. Then there were things we didn't typically think about, like the way we wanted to speak to our kids. We communicated with them not as babies, but as humans. Smart and conscious communication with our children was important to us. We thought it was important to teach them about expectations and boundaries. We talked about the kind of discipline we were going to use with them. Each of these traits all roll back to the 5 Essentials that are important in every relationship, and the reason for this book. See how important they are? Our children are no different.

While growing a human inside of you is a miracle, it's the growth they do on the outside as individuals that takes the most work. Being aware of the kind of parent you want to be and taking the job of imparting your knowledge and wisdom on them is one of our biggest responsibilities. I don't know about you, but I take my mom job very seriously. Making sure my kids have the 5 Essentials in their lives so they are aware of how to cultivate and maintain their relationships is one of the best gifts I can give them. I mean, in the end all we can ask for is to do the best job we can and for our kids to do the same. Leading by example is how you do it.

## BECAUSE... *Learning to Communicate with Your Kid & Partner!*

We are not mind readers, although it might be a cool super power. Just like having to work on communication with your partner, you also have to do it with your kids (and all the other relationships in your life). When you're a parent, it takes a while to get to know the language your children speak. When they're babies, they have different sounds to let you know what they need and you get the fun job of deciphering them. Are they hungry? Tired? Poopy? As they get older they eventually learn how to speak for themselves which is their cue for us to start teaching them how to communicate effectively.

I started talking to my babes early. Like seriously talking to them. And not in that God forsaken baby voice. What if someone talked to you like that? How would you feel? I used a calm, rhythmic voice so they get used to it. Baby talk only lasts a minute in the grand scheme of things, and it's totally annoying to hear a grown adult talking to a toddler in baby voice. Sorry, it just is.

When you become parents, you learn quickly that you need to clearly communicate your expectations. In order for the family to do well on the day-to-day, get clear on how you want to parent FIRST. Then start parenting. I highly recommend getting on the same page about decisions early on, then you don't have to deal with them moment by moment. Having open dialogue with the person you're parenting with is the most important element in raising kids. It doesn't matter if you're still together as a couple, but it matters that you're raising your kids together.

Expectation setting is a great thing to start doing before your kids arrive.

Will you be the kind of parents who have each other's backs when the going gets tough with your kids? (I sure hope so!) Or will you be manipulated by them? It totally happens and we all know people who allow their kids to dictate their lives. If you're not on the same page with your co-parent *most* of the time, then your kids will be running the show. That's not what you, or they, want to have happen. Even if they think they do. Being honest with your kids and open with your communication with them from day one helps create strong self-confident people.

Managing expectations with our family hasn't always been easy. I especially (any other ladies out there??) forget that my partner is not a mind reader. I had to remember to be very clear about my expectations with Will, and where I really needed his help. I can remember when this actually hit home for me.

It was on my wedding anniversary. I don't remember which one, but probably around year 14. The kids were play fighting in their bedroom not listening to me tell them one of them was bound to get hurt. Neither one of them had eaten their dinner, yet they were both lobbying for dessert. My husband wasn't home yet and when he did come home, I was putting away laundry. His greeting to me was, "Hi, happy anniversary. Your flowers are on the table." That's when I lost it. I sat on the bed and started to cry. I mean, the first thought that went through my head was, "You seriously couldn't walk the flowers into the bedroom to say happy anniversary?" And now, in the background one of my boys was crying because OF COURSE he got hurt play fighting like I said he would. It was complete chaos and I was breaking.

Let me preface this by saying, these feelings had been a long time coming. Because I am who I am, I tend to take on a lot of stuff until I break. Until I'm basically drowning and am forced to ask for help. So now I'm sitting there crying, my kids are crying and my husband is freaked out. All I kept saying over and over was, "I can't do this anymore." He had no idea what I was talking about. Happy Anniversary.

You see, up until that moment, I had been doing everything. Working full time, managing the kids, making the dinners, maintaining our home and all the other things that come with it. My husband went to work and came home. He took out the garbage and helped with the kids on weekends. Because of his work schedule, he isn't typically home until after dinner, when bath time commences. It's a lot for one person to deal with day in and day out, but that's just how it is. Or so I thought. As I was having my breakdown, all he wanted to know was how he could help me. What did I need? Whatever it was, he would do it. Then he said this, "You have to tell me what you expect from me because if you don't I won't know. I can't read your mind." What?! Lightbulb!!

After that night, I told him and the kids I needed them to pitch in more, and help out around the house. Incredibly, because I asked for what I needed, and was clear about my expectations, everything changed. It wasn't a knock down drag out fight, it was a conversation. Once we hashed it out, everything started working. Everyone started being more considerate of each other, and taking the initiative to pitch in more. PLEASE, communicate your expectations with your partner and your kids. This will alleviate so much stress you can't even imagine. It's a true game changer. Look what it did for me!

## BECAUSE... *Kids Will Test All The Boundaries!*

Children are strong willed and will test your every last nerve. I can remember the first (and basically only) time Wyatt was put in time out. He was 2, and it was one of the worst days ever. He was not listening, and was throwing tantrums and driving my husband and I crazy. It was the day of the NYC Marathon. We live in a neighborhood in Brooklyn where the runners go directly down our main avenue. It's quite an event down on the street. We enjoy watching and cheering on the runners.

That year our son was not having it. We went out, but he wasn't listening. It was not enjoyable for anyone. So, we took him home to try to nap him — to no avail. I can remember being so frustrated by his actions that I was literally shaking when I put him in time out. We were both crying. It was awful. He finally cried himself to sleep, and I followed suit with a nap of my own. The whole episode drained me completely. He woke up a happy baby.

Later, I remember asking him how it felt to be in trouble. He said, "No good." After that day he has rarely been punished. I think it traumatized us both for a long time. This was one of the biggest kid tests of my boundaries to date.

This forced me to learn a LOT about myself. It tested my patience to the limit. I hated having to punish my child (and I learned that I'm not good at it.) I also learned that time-outs don't work for my family. This is precisely why I believe that constantly communicating with the other parent and the kids is so important.

After this terrible day, we found a different way to deal with punishment that was so much more effective.

I was having a conversation with a few of my girlfriends recently. One is a mother of girls, the other boys. We were talking about the differences in raising boys, vs raising girls — and how they definitely both push boundaries — they just do it differently. Mostly we were talking about some of the things that have surprised us. Like for instance, lying.

One of my friend's daughter's lied to her for an entire marking period of school. She had been telling her mom that she had completed her homework. Come to find out that she had never turned in one assignment! These kids are in the fifth grade. As a mother of a child that age, I would expect a call from the teacher after a few missed assignments just to make sure everything was ok at home. Alas, in this case, that did not happen.

In walk two unsuspecting parents for their child's parent/teacher conference. They were expecting more of the same about their daughter as they had heard in past meetings. Instead they got smacked with the fact that their sweet, smart daughter had been lying to them for* weeks! No bueno my friends! Isn't it funny? For as mad as we can get at them, we forgive them, we discipline them, and we never stop loving them.

Have you ever gotten pushed so far by your sweet babies that you wanted to throw in the towel? Ever wanted to drop the handful of toys and walk out the door to peace and quiet (and maybe a glass of wine)? If your answer is no, I'm calling you out. I don't believe you. We have all had days where we question why we became a parent. Moments when we are brought to the brink of our ability to hold it together.

I offend my mother every time she asks me if I could imagine my life without my kids — because my answer is a resounding YES. I can. I had a really great life before they came along. I often pull up memories of those days. Now if she asked me the question differently perhaps in the form of, "Can you imagine your future without your kids?" Then my answer is a resounding NO, I cannot. I don't regret one day with them. I might want a do over every once in a while but no regrets.

## BECAUSE... *Kids Need The Essentials Too!*

In due time, when I write the #WhyAmIYelling? Because...*Parenting* book, I'll go into a lot more detail about this stuff, but for the purposes of this book, touching on it is the goal. I'm including the parenting angle because I have two kids at home and I'm in the middle of it. The biggest thing that I want to remind all people in their relationships with these smaller humans, is that kids need the 5 Essentials too. Just as much as we do — if not more.

Back when we were kids, without realizing it, we really just wanted our parents to say to see us, acknowledge us as people and say, "Hey, I get it. This is not an easy time for you. Let's figure it out together." Or something like that. In reality, I'm not sure many of us got that. I don't think an emphasis was put on communication at the time I was growing up. I think it was more of a, "If it ain't broke, then don't fix it," kind of mentality. The 5 Essentials encourage a different way.

I think kids these days are fighting for attention from their peers and parents in our very competitive world. Keeping the communication lines open is the most important thing I can do for my children. Reminding them that I'm there for them with subtle hints and affection can make or break their day. It's my job to pay attention, and learn their patterns.

Sometimes they will open up at the oddest moments. We do a lot of our talking at bedtime. Our nightly ritual is for us to all lay in bed and talk about our day. We each take turns talking about what was great and not so great about it. It's in these moments, with the lights off, that my boys like to take advantage of having in depth conversations. Nothing is off limits and their comfort levels are increased. I take those opportunities when they come and run with them. I give them the attention and respect they deserve. Even when the topic may feel difficult for me to hear, I do my very best to listen to them. I don't interrupt. My job is to be a sounding board.

Once my boys realized they had my ear and my undying support, they've been more apt to continue the communication as they've grown. Creating good communication habits with kids helps us all get through those hard conversations. It also teaches them to have strong communication habits throughout their lives.

Along with communication comes the rest of the 5 Essentials. Respect, Support, Intimacy and Boundaries. I know I talked about them above but I really want to drive this point home. I love my children and I show them that love frequently. I work hard to create a home for them to feel safe in, where they can be who they truly are, without judgement. It's hard enough being a kid, I don't want to make it harder. I keep that in mind when I'm spending time with mine. How about you?

When it comes to our kids, Will and I simply want to make sure they are getting the most well- rounded experiences we can provide as their parents. Education, family time, extracurricular activities, travel, and allowing them their own independence are super important to us. We incorporate the Essentials into our daily lives, and it works well for us. It's also reduced our need to punish — which — as I've said — I hate so much!

Every generation is different. I only hope the way we are choosing to teach our kids is something they will appreciate and take with them as they grow. I'm grateful to be parenting kids in this crazy world. I'm excited for their futures (and mine) as they continue to expand and explore. If you work at having a successful relationship with your kids through the 5 Essentials, they are most likely going to continue those loving and valuable skills through their adulthood.

*Raising a family takes a lot of work. It takes dedication, love and a huge amount of understanding. You are teaching your kids to be productive, good humans as they grow, and you are growing right alongside of them. Cherish your time with your kids, I realize how significant every single experience is because they are fleeting. You will never get the special moments back, so make sure you are paying attention. It's an honor to be a parent, remember to treat it as such.*

## BECAUSE...
# Friendships!

What would we do without our friends? I would die. Seriously. Die. I need my friends in a big way. In order to have meaningful friendships, I have been spending my lifetime using and refining the 5 Essentials here too. All of our relationships take work and that includes our friendships, no matter which kind they are.

Friendships come in a lot of different shapes and sizes and for me, each of my friendships has a different meaning, special memory and place in my life. Some friends are closer. Some friends come as whole groups. Some friends I love deeply, but only see once every 5 years.

My girlfriends from my early days were my guiding light in setting friendship standards for myself. My mom friends are my beacons of hope and joy in the club of parenthood. My guy friends provide different perspective on life in general. My lifelong friends are my rocks. Sure, some of my friendships have fallen by the wayside. Some of my friendships have ceased to exist. All of this is part of life for each of us. Each of them should be appreciated. That's exactly what we'll do now.

Let's talk about our friends.

# BECAUSE... We Need Our Grown-Up Girlfriends!

I want to start this chapter by paying homage to my mother. I mean let's face it, I learned how to do friendship from her. My first real memory of true friendship was watching my mother in hers. It wasn't necessarily her guiding me, but more of me observing through the years the importance she placed on her friendships. To this day, my mother has friendships that are as old, and maybe older than me. I'm in the second half of my 40's, those are some long friendships! I have a lot of mad respect for my mom and how she taught me to appreciate the value of friendship.

Earlier in the book I talked a lot about my adolescent friendships, and why they were important. Now I want to talk about the importance of having a solid group of girlfriends as we grow older. There's a difference. As a youngster, I was more impressionable and less comfortable in my own skin. I was more likely to agree with my friend's opinions, so as to not rock the boat. As I've gotten older I've realized that my friends will still love me for who I am — despite our differences. Or maybe they love me because of them. Ever think of that for your own relationships?

I find that as I've gotten older I'm drawn to women who are strong minded, and not afraid to speak about their beliefs and values. They are secure in themselves, open-hearted and are willing to see differences in perspective. Those girlfriends are the ones who keep me in check. I didn't necessarily pick friends like this as a younger woman.

I've been reflecting on my friendships a lot as I write this book. The friendships you have as adults are very different from the ones you have as kids. They're deeper and more meaningful. They are full of life experience and learning lessons. And if you're lucky, they are not full of judgement. The girlfriends I have in my life right now at this moment are some of the most amazing women I have ever had the pleasure of knowing. They have gotten me through some of my hardest days and have cheered me through some of my best days. They are a constant in my life and for that I am humbled and grateful.

The most valuable part of my friendships these days is the difference in perspective that I have from each of my friends. None of us look at a situation the same way — which is remarkable and refreshing all at the same time. While we may want the same outcome of a particular situation, we may take different paths to get there. Case in point, I met a new friend a few years ago when I was traveling to a conference in Florida. I was flying solo on that trip, and I was crazy nervous to be putting myself and my new business out there without a wingman. I'm not sure how I got up the courage to do it, but I bought my ticket to the event, got on a plane and acted like I knew what I was doing.

About three hours into the first day of the conference, I was sitting on a comfy chair checking my messages between speaking sessions, when a woman sat down opposite me and we started chatting. Turns out it was her first conference too! She was from North Carolina and could not be sweeter or funnier. We hit it off immediately. By the end of the three days we were thick as thieves, and continue to be from afar.

While we were together on that trip, I learned that we couldn't be more different on paper. Yet, at our cores we are very similar.

I think that's part of why our friendship is the way it is. We can appreciate our differences and have thought provoking conversations, without argument. It's more important for us to be supportive and understanding, especially now, at this stage of our lives. We're both mothers, business owners and voices for others. Being mindful of how we are presenting ourselves can really help in the perspective department.

When I talk about my adult girlfriends, this is what I mean. We can share our ideas and beliefs and even when we disagree, we can still love one another. We can appreciate each other's opinions, and be a support system. It's important to have friends like this in your life. Friends you can lean on, share your secrets with and turn to in good times and bad. These people are my lifeline.

The other biggest difference between my girlfriends of the current day verses my younger years is empathy. Good God, when I see a friend struggling, I go to the place that's right there with her. I'm not sure if a switch flips when you get to a certain age, but man, since I've become a more seasoned human, my sensitivity has heightened toward others. When you're an adolescent kid, you're mostly selfish, I see it with a lot of kids these days including my own children. Yes, they are empathetic to a degree, but mostly they're focused on their own personal outcome of a situation, putting themselves first. And while there's nothing wrong with that, at that particular stage, it really is life changing when you learn the lesson that the world does not revolve around you.

Being a good friend is having the ability to encourage, support and expose your true self to your tribe and be accepted for it. The 5 Essentials are teaching us that throughout these pages. When you allow yourself to open up with your girlfriends and let them into your inner circle of feelings, desires and needs, your entire world can change. One of the best things about having true friends is the fact that you can do you and you'll still be loved and appreciated at the end of the day.

Like I said, I have been very fortunate to have had a solid sisterhood throughout my life. But especially now, in the times when my life has been the most topsy-turvy, I appreciate my friends so much. Knowing I have a squad to fall back on to lend an ear, pick up a kid when I'm in a bind, let loose when I'm feeling stressed or simply celebrate for no particular reason is a true joy. I hope my friends feel the same way about me, and I hope you have a tribe that fulfills all of that for you.

## BECAUSE... *Real Friends Don't Judge!*

Good friends aren't judgmental. Are they opinionated? Yes. But when it comes right down to it, they will support you in the end no matter what. When Will and I first started dating, I caught a log of judgement from my parents about how he looked and what his choice of profession was. A bartender with long hair, multiple piercings in his ears, and a tattoo on his ankle. He was not the image of the prince charming my parents had in their heads. It didn't matter that he was crazy smart, loved their daughter and was a genuinely nice guy. That was probably the lowest time in my relationship with my parents on so many levels. The truth about their superficial judgement shocked me to my core along with the fact that they were basically forcing me to choose between him and them. I can remember telling my mother point blank after a fight that he was the man I was going to marry and that she would eventually see him and love him.

That time in my life was so hard and I leaned on my friends like never before. Late night phone calls, long talks and lots of love and support came from them without one ounce of judgement. That was really the first time I wasn't supported by my family and while it sucked, it also gave me a new point of view. My rose-colored glasses had shattered, and my girlfriends helped me get through an extremely difficult time in my life.

As I've gotten older and cultivated friendships in a few different circles, the one theme I'm continually coming across is the importance of the non-judgmental support system we are creating. None of us is without a personal struggle and because we all know and understand that it, we have to be able to lean each other when we need an ear or an opinion. I'm not saying opinions can't be different, that's a given in some cases. What I'm talking about is when you have a friend that can hear your plight, and create a safe space for you to feel comfortable sharing yourself with them. That's when your friendship creates lasting bonds.

A lot of my friends are moms. We're all raising our kids together and learning as we go together, which is a huge gift. Each of us has a different life situation, which I look at as an opportunity to learn from rather than criticize. If one of my friends is doing something different from me in their parenting or marriage, I want to know why and how it's beneficial. I don't want to drag them down for something I may not be interested in for my family. How could I possibly judge another parent's decisions when they're two completely different dynamics?

I was recently interviewed for a the Dad AF Podcast. We were talking about parenting and one of the questions I was asked was "What is your least favorite thing about parenting?" My answer, without hesitation, is judgmental mothers. Lord knows they're out there, and we need to end that shit. Instead of judgment, how about love? Instead of superiority, how about support? I know it's so easy to judge, but we have no idea what that other person is dealing with on the daily.

This brings me to a recent discussion I was having with several of my mom friends at one of our much-needed nights out. We were talking about our adolescent children (shocker) and how different they all are with their schooling, interests and growth patterns. One of my girlfriends admitted her child was struggling with school and was lashing out. This behavior was of course made her question the way she and her husband were parenting their child. She was frustrated, upset and concerned for her kiddo, and at the same time beating herself up internally for being a bad mom.

It didn't take two seconds before the rest of our group started to chime in with support and love for our dear friend who was trying to navigate these delicate waters without losing her shit. There were suggestions for tools they could use and ideas for professional intervention. Most importantly there was nothing but love at that table. Not one ounce of judgement, because we need less of that in the world.

Being a form of support is one of the most important pieces of friendship and relationships overall (5 Essentials anyone?). Think about your friendships. Are you feeling loved for who you are — without judgement? If so, take stock in how fortunate you are to have a group of people who love you for who you are, and nothing more or less. If you are not feeling that, it's time to start creating that for you. A network of supporters there to help you along your way. That stuff is life changing.

## BECAUSE... *Guy Friends Rule!*

It's no secret that I love men. Men make me feel good, confident, strong, sexy, smart. That is of course if I'm surrounding myself with the right ones. I've been fortunate in my life to have many men who've been childhood friends, co-workers or friends of friends become very special people in my life. They're all really awesome. Here's the thing though, especially today with all of the #MeToo work going on, we are in danger of losing platonic relationships between men and women.

My men friends are becoming increasingly scared that they will be accused of doing the wrong thing or of having a comment or a physical interaction misunderstood. We have to be very careful when we're navigating these waters, no doubt. However, we cannot be so guarded that we miss the natural beauty of a relationship.

I mean, if I'm being honest, I've got plenty of my own #MeToo moments to throw in the bucket. None were assault related, thank God, but I'm no stranger to inappropriate comments or advances. I spoke about it earlier in the book. It was one of the reasons I left my corporate job years ago. So I'm in no way trying to diminish the message because it's extremely important. I'm merely saying it is also important to remember that not every man is a misogynistic dick. Most of them are not. One bad apple shouldn't spoil it for the whole bunch, ya know what I'm sayin?

I'm a big believer in opposite sex friendships. My guy friends have provided me with lots of great advice, different perspectives, and help throughout my years. That's why I think having a variety of types of friends is important. It's good to get a different perspective

185

on things when needed. It has nothing to do with attraction and everything to do with a genuine affinity for another human being, regardless of gender. It often gets my goat when other women say things like, "My husband doesn't like it that I have male friends," or "I think it's disrespectful to my husband to have other men as friends in my life." That's just plain hogwash.

I'm not sure how I came to be a woman who has a good number of guys for friends. Maybe it's because I happen to love sports? Maybe it's because I worked in a male dominated corporate setting for a long time? Or maybe it's just because I'm an outgoing person who enjoys good conversation and company? But these friendships are just as important to me as my female friends. Just a little bit different.

I have a ton of great memories that I've made with my guy friends. Tailgating at NY Giants games, going to playoff games at Yankee Stadium, concerts at Madison Square Garden, annual steak house dinners, too many to count! These events are not only fun but they're meaningful in a way that makes me feel appreciated. Granted, now that I have two kids and my life has gone in a completely different direction, I will admit that it's gotten harder to hang with my dudes. But whenever the opportunity arises, I make myself available. Case in point, I have a dear friend for many years. This a man I used to work with, who will reach out every time he's in the city for work to see if we can get together for dinner. Now, I'm fully aware he could just hop on a train and go home after what typically is a hectic day for him, but he makes the choice to spend a few hours catching up with an old friend.

One of my favorite stories with this particular friend was the time I crashed his annual corporate sales conference in Las Vegas. Yep. I went to Vegas with a guy I wasn't married to, and my husband was cool with it. Relax. It wasn't like that. Hear me out.

One night I'm out for drinks with a bunch of my former coworkers and the topic of Vegas comes up. One of the guys says to me and another female friend of ours, "Hey, I'm going to Vegas tomorrow for my annual sales kick-off. You guys should come." To which we responded, "We should," in unison. That literally got the ball rolling. It was a matter of minutes before my girlfriend and I were on the phone to our respective husbands clearing the way for us to go to Vegas with our mutual guy friend. While we were working our magic, our friend was booking flights for us for the next day. Seriously. Within two hours we had booked a trip to Vegas, confirmed that we would crash with our male friend and whoop it up for two, or was it three nights… Who can remember? We ran home, packed a quick bag and were on a flight ten hours later. We had THE BEST time!! And yes, what happens in Vegas, stays in Vegas.

Now I realize that this type of experience is not the norm — which is why it was so great! It was spontaneous, fun and harmless. It was a few days of having a great time with good friends. There were no expectations, no drama and lots of laughs and drinks! To this day, every time I'm reminded of Vegas, I smile from that great memory.

That's why I love having guys in my life who I can call true friends because it's easy. They make friendship easy for me. I can't possibly put into words how important that is.

I think men and women just naturally approach friendship differently. That's what makes my guy friendships so refreshing, and feel so easy. They don't involve work. They just want to hang out and have some laughs. In my case, when I've truly needed a different perspective of the male perspective, other than my husbands, I will lean on my guy friends for their opinion without fear of judgement. Men are really good at taking circumstances at face value, something women struggle with.

So, I thank you, my guys, for being a source of support, fun and honesty when I've truly needed you. You've made me a better friend, wife and mother. I appreciate you all so much.

## BECAUSE... *Life Long Friends!*

Consider yourself very lucky if you have friends in your life from a time when you can't really remember them not being there. I can count on one hand these friends of mine. They are the ones I will call first when I need a shoulder or an ear. They're the ones who have known me the longest. We've been through all the breakups, makeups, babies, marriages, divorces, deaths, sicknesses, you name it there's probably not a subject we haven't experienced through one another. These are the friends who would drop everything and bail you out of jail if you needed them to. I have a few of those.

Two of my oldest friends are from my adolescent years. We met in Florida as disgruntled tweenagers, hung around in the same circles and had most of the same classes together in high school. We all went to different colleges, yet we made it a point to visit one another and spend time together during mutual breaks from school. Were we inseparable when we were kids? No. In fact I would say that while we spent time together, there were other friends who I spent more time with. But for some reason the universe thought it would be good idea for us to all remain friends to this day — thirty something years later and going strong. We still talk all the time, bring our families together and consult frequently with each other for parenting advice. We are still really close.

If you're lucky enough to have friends like this then you know what I'm talking about. Having people in your life that you can count on no matter what is comforting. Even though we live in different places, we find time to visit one another and chat via

189

phone or text. There's something about having friendships that can stand the test of time that I am particularly proud of.

When I think of lifelong friends, I think of the people who show up time and time again. Not only for the good stuff but for the knock the wind out of you stuff too. The friends who don't ask questions, they come in and take over if needed. Again, I'll refer here back to my mom and her lifelong friendships. When my father passed away her friends swooped in and took over. They cooked, cleaned and got my mom out of the house when I couldn't be there. It's been over a year since my dad's been gone and mom still has daily interaction with her core friends. In my case, my lifelong friends did the same for me at that time. They showed up. They supported. They loved.

Lifelong friendships aren't always lollipops and rainbows. It's the fact that when you do disagree, you can do it in a mature and responsible way. By having real, honest conversations about how you're feeling. By hashing out issues, maybe with one another or maybe to get an opinion on a different situation, but always with an open mind and ear. I sustain these relationships because of our mutual admiration and respect for one another. Because I have a genuine love for these people that I consider my family.

Lifelong friendships are a gift and should be treated as such. You will never have another friend like the ones that have been around since your beginning. If you are lucky enough have cultivated these, be grateful for them and acknowledge how utterly fantastic it is to be loved in this way!

# BECAUSE... *Friends That Got Away!*

We all have them, right? The friendships that lasted years and then for one reason or another, they just kind of go by the wayside. Well, I have one or two of those. When I think back on those specific friendships I realize it was one of two things. Either a matter of timing, where we were in different phases of our lives, or it was that the friendship had run its course and was no longer serving one or both of us.

The friendship I want to discuss is someone I still keep in peripheral touch with thanks to social media. We're friends on Facebook and all that, so we occasionally comment on one another's photos and revel in how much time has really passed since we last spoke or saw one another. So, she didn't really get all that far away. But, we aren't as close as we used to be. It is very simply that this friendship is the classic case of us being in two different phases of our lives.

When we met, I was in my 20's. We worked together and hung out together. She was 10 years older than me, and she was married. At the time, I was not. She was planning on having a family. I think she may have been in the early stages of her first pregnancy. I was nowhere near that phase of my life, yet we forged a great bond. I lived with her during her first pregnancy because her husband was in the military, and he was deployed at the time. There were birthdays, weekend trips to the Florida Keys, and dinner parties at her house. Once her first child was born I spent a lot of time being present in their lives.

They would go on to have three amazing kids whose lives I was a significant part of in their early years. They moved a few times.

This made it harder to see each other. I made the effort to visit and spend time with them because that was a priority for me. When my life took a new turn, with marriage and kids of my own, I had to make choices based on my family's needs. Our vacations would be to see grandparents instead of visiting far away friends. The timing of life happens differently for some. Especially when you move away from each other. That's what happened to this particular friendship. She got away because of life and timing.

It doesn't mean we're not still friends, or that we wouldn't hang out if circumstances were different. To me it means our friendship was significant for the time it needed to be. It served its main purpose when it was available. It's okay for a friendship to mature and serve a purpose. Not all friendships will last forever, and that's okay. I will never discount that friendship. Like I said, she's not really gone. We still exchange Christmas cards, are friends on Facebook and I can tell you that if we're ever in one another's vicinities, we would reach out. That friendship will rekindle if and when it serves us both. The universe knows it.

My other experience when it comes to friends getting away is with the friendships that are no longer serving you. I know none of us are immune to the friendship break up experience. Quite frankly, it sucks when you finally realize that a particular friendship is draining you, or not filling you up. I had to break up with a friend for this reason. It was hard. Really hard. But, unfortunately, it was for the best in the long run.

Have you ever had a friend who only reaches out when they need something? Or when you're together they're spending their time bashing other "friends" and talking mainly about themselves? I mean, yes, we've all been selfish at points with our friends, especially if we're going through a personal situation, but in this case, I'm talking about when you're out for a fun brunch and within five minutes you feel like the life is being sucked out of you. If you're nodding after reading that sentence, then you know.

It took me a long time to realize that I wasn't being fulfilled in that particular friendship. Or perhaps I chose to put my blinders on because that friendship was part of a bigger group of friends who spent time together. Whatever it was, I was clearly avoiding the issue and it eventually started to bother me. I needed to figure out why I was feeling the way I was and how to approach the discussion with my friend. This was not familiar ground for me, I've never had to break up with a friend before!

I started to notice things in our friendship feeling more one sided and that wasn't sitting well with me. I would show up for her whenever she needed me to, but when I needed her, she wasn't available, or would cancel our plans. I found myself making excuses for why our friendship was the way it was until I realized that she was not putting me on the same priority level as I was putting her. That went on for quite a while, a few years, before I realized it was something I had to address.

Let me say this — I hate confrontation of any kind. I get emotional, scared and nervous. I am not a good arguer. In recent years I've gotten much better at learning how to let things go through using meditation practice. But this situation happened before I found my zen, so it was particularly uncomfortable.

I had met my friend for drinks and in typical fashion, the conversation was about someone else who wasn't falling into line with what my friend wanted. Of course that person was on her shit list. After listening for a bit, I was so worked up in my head, and reacting to what she was saying, that I literally told her to stop talking while she was mid-sentence. I'm not normally abrupt, so naturally, she was taken off guard. I needed to do it that way for her to hear me.

I will say this, our conversation never got heated. I asked for her to listen, and laid out my feelings and perceptions. I asked her for her opinion and views of our friendship, and while we agreed to a few differences, we just could not come together on others.

It was a hard conversation. A friend break-up can be worse that breaking up with a romantic partner. I mean, boyfriends come and go. True friendships can last a lifetime. We both realized then that this was not one of those friendships. And while I don't regret that particular experience, I recognize it could only serve either one of us for so long. Welcome to adulthood.

I've seen this happen not only through personal experience, but with my friends and family as well. I've watched generations-long friendships fizzle for many different reasons. Sometimes friendships are too exhausting to continue to commit to. Personality differences, priorities and attitude go a long way when you're maintaining a relationship with another person. As we age, our priorities shift and being around people who are a constant energy suck, can be damaging to you, and to your self-esteem. Even the ones we think are going to stand the test of time. The friendship we invested in many years ago may not be the same friendship today. We grow and evolve regularly which means our relationships have to do the same. Sometimes that works, and sometimes it doesn't.

Not every friendship is built to be lifelong. Each one has its own special significance. As I get older I am more aware and particular about the people I choose to invite into my inner circle. I don't have time to be friends with everyone the way I once did. Being choosy should be something we do when we're cultivating friendships. We should want to be compatible with the people we plan on being around for extended periods of time. Relationships are all about quality, not quantity.

I think the learning lesson for me when it comes to the friendships that got away is that we shouldn't dwell on the why's or what ifs. I simply appreciate the time we spent and enjoyed with one another. I mean, who knows, in another space and time there may be room to rekindle an old friendship. Just because it isn't something that works right now doesn't mean it won't work later.

*Like I said earlier, friendships come in all shapes and sizes and you have to do the work in order to keep them healthy and strong. For me, having solid friendships throughout my life has been one of my greatest accomplishments. I don't take friendship lightly, it's a bond that I am actively creating with another human being and that's a big deal. Friendship should be appreciated and acknowledged, especially as we get older because we are more aware of how special it is. Take stock in your friendships and be thankful for them because there are some that you couldn't live without.*

## BECAUSE...

# The Death of a Relationship!

It never occurred to me to discuss the grieving of a relationship in detail as I was initially writing this book. Then during the preliminary editing stages, my father passed away. Losing a relationship was now so front and center in my life, that I had the pull to write about it. In fact, it's still pretty fresh as I type these words. I'm sure I'm still only in the beginning stages of the grieving process but I would be remiss to not talk about it because it's a thing.

Grieving the loss of a close relationship is tough. But, as nothing is permanent, it's a reality that we face again and again as humans. Having to let relationships and people go from our lives is an unavoidable part of life. I can remember being a young girl and crying over losing a boyfriend after a breakup, or a friend after a disagreement. Every sad pang in my stomach from the memories that came up made me feel like I got the wind knocked out of me. I thought that was hard. These disappointments were nothing like the loss of my father.

My parents had a miracle of a marriage. They spent 55 years together. They were kids when they started dating, hell they were kids when they got married. They experienced life together. They grew up together. When my father died, we all wondered, as you do, what would happen next? Would mom be able to handle her grief? How would our family dynamic change? So. Many. Questions. Then there's the logistical stuff, which is way easier said than done. Luckily for us, mom is a rock and while she has her daily moments, she has continued to be a shining example of strength surrounded by her friends and loved ones every day.

Now that it's been more than a year since his passing, I've had the time to process and come to terms with it. I initially wanted to write about dad's funeral, how our family and friends came together in a way that I had never seen before. And unfortunately, I've been to my share of funerals. I was going to give you the details of his send off — from the open bar at his viewing (yes, that did happen and I have the koozie to prove it) — to the bag-pipes playing in the front of the church as the hearse drove away from us. But those details aren't what's important here. What's important for this final part of the book is to understand and accept when a relationship is final. And by final, I mean there is no way you can ever get it back. Death is involved.

You may have past relationships that you are not planning on rekindling, and that's fine. But in the back of your mind you know that person is still alive. If that's the case, the possibility to patch things up still exists. But when someone you love passes on, whether it's suddenly or expected, there will likely come a point in your grieving process when you will eventually be okay with it. Where you will find closure and peace if you are seeking it. They key is to want it. If you are, or have gone through this recently, I want to tell you that I understand. I know what you are going through. I send you my deep love and assistance in processing your loss. Please give yourself the time you need to heal.

For some of us that will be one of the most difficult things we've ever had to do. In my case, with my father, I found the process to be gradual and comforting at the same time. After the funeral I was talking to one of my friends and she asked if I felt like an orphan. My answer to that is no. Because I'm not. BUT, I do have a friend who is and we talked about her situation recently.

She is one of many siblings. And for some reason, after her parent's deaths, the kids all scattered. She called her father the glue that held the family together. In this case literally. When he passed, it seemed to her that the family values changed. Spending time together with sisters and brothers wasn't a priority any longer. Making the effort to be together for holidays and gatherings stopped.

On some levels, jealousy about personal situations, successes, and meaningless stuff got in the way. Now she doesn't speak to any of her siblings except one brother. That makes me sad and it makes me want to fix it. It makes me want to reach out to all of them (even though I don't know them) to find out root causes, and talk about the importance of forgiveness and letting go. I want to talk of not harboring resentment and bad feelings, especially over dumb shit. And in the end, it's all dumb shit.

You aren't always going to agree with your family and friends. That's natural. But, if you have the core of your relationship intact (the 5 Essentials hm, hmmmm), a relationship can weather almost any situation. You guys, that's the beauty of relationships and opinions, we all have them. The question is how tolerant are we? How willing are we to accept a difference of opinion to move on through love?

I think about my friend's situation, and I wonder if she's truly as okay with not seeing her family as she claims she is. I wonder if she feels closure about her parents passing when she thinks and talks about it. I know she has a big heart and I know she's been hurt, and has probably hurt her siblings. Let's face it, there are three sides to every story, right? Family stuff is hard, we all have it, no one is immune to it.

Another question that popped up in the wake of my father's passing was the question of unfinished business. Was I satisfied with the status of our relationship upon his passing? Were there things that were left unsaid? More thoughts to provoke!! My answer to that is yes, I was happy with things between us when he passed.

While we didn't necessarily see eye to eye on a few things throughout my life, essentially the important ones are the ones that matter. At the end of the day, I know he loved me. I know he was proud of the life I had chosen to lead. He loved the husband I was blessed with, even though the beginning was a little rocky. He loved the grandchildren we blessed him with, who called him grandpa. That's the stuff that matters. I love that we were able to accept our differences. Even though we may not have agreed on some levels, we rarely argued about them because we knew better than to engage in the discussion. Our time together was limited mostly due to geography, so when we were together, we chose to focus on the stuff that mattered.

How do you get that closure if there are things unsaid, and the person has passed? How do you achieve it?

The important part of closure is that you work to move on without resentment, or the feeling of having unfinished business. Sometimes we have to go back and revisit a relationship to achieve that. Sometimes we can't and we have to accept and work through the questions we have that are centered around it. This becomes its most true when death occurs.

Of course, in the circumstance of death, well, that's something entirely different but it's not something I think is lost altogether. I'm a big believer in angels. I talk to them all day long. I know I have a few in my corner. Call it what you will, but if there's someone out there who's no longer with you, and you have unfinished business and need closure, talk to them. Ask them for a sign, tell them how you feel and why you feel it. I bet you'll feel different when you're finished. My hope is that you feel relieved of your burden. I bet you feel some type of closure. This is always available to you. And who knows, you may have acquired an angel in the process.

Moving forward after the loss of a relationship will never be easy. I don't care if you couldn't wait for it to end. I don't care if it was the worst thing you've ever experienced. I don't care if it was the greatest thing on the planet. It's still not easy. Moving on is a choice, just like everything else in our lives. Making the choice to move forward, hell even remembering that you HAVE the choice to move forward, is empowering.

It might take time to realize that, it often does. The tunnel will probably feel dark and lonely at times, maybe even claustrophobic, but there is light at the end of it. I promise you that there is. Moving forward is a learning experience. It's cathartic. It's hard. Death is such a transformative process for everyone involved, that it may even make you a different person.

## BECAUSE... *All Relationships Take Work!*

Woo Hoo! You've officially made it through the relationships with others part of this book! In this section we've explored the ins and outs of having relationships on every level from adolescence to adulthood. I explored firsts, shared some embarrassing moments and told you about significant times in not only my life, but lives I've been touched by. The underlying theme through sharing these stories is that every relationship takes work. By putting in the work, through practicing the 5 Essentials, you are making a conscious effort to create successful, loving relationships with all of the people in your life. Keep up the great work!

## BECANSE...

# What I Know!

Phew!! You made it to the end of the book!! I wasn't sure how I wanted to end it — I mean, I felt like ending with death could be too emotional, so I decided to do a little recap of all of the things I've learned through my eight hundred years on earth when it comes to relationships. Being the optimist that I am in all areas of my life, I truly do believe I have the power to create my story. I believe you do too.

And now without further ado, here's what I know.

It may sound cliche' and I hope it doesn't because I truly mean it. You only get one go-round at this thing we call life. One. And while it may seem difficult at times, and there will be days you won't want to get out of bed to face it, know this — life is a gift. It truly is. The way you choose to live it is entirely up to you. In a nutshell, here is how I choose to live the gift of life.

Make good choices. You will have many relationships through-out your life. In each one you will have the opportunity to create something amazing or not. That's the beauty of having a choice.

Believe in yourself. Your thoughts, opinions and feelings matter. Don't ever let another person tell you otherwise.

Be fearless. Learn something new every day. Ask for help. Find your passion and run with it. Make sure you are fearless in your relationships too.

Piss people off — it's okay. The relationships that are supposed to survive it will.

Acknowledge your mistakes. Own your shit. Being able to say you're sorry in your relationships is a huge strength.

Stand for what you believe in. Never back down — your voice should be heard. This is imperative in all of your relationships.

Give from your heart. Love unconditionally. Expect nothing in return. You're in for a rude awakening if you expect more than you give in your relationships.

Travel. Do it alone because it feeds your soul and do it with others because it truly is amazing to see wonder through another person's eyes.

When you choose to do all of these things, your world will open up, your mind will expand and your relationships will thrive. I know this.

Xo

# Acknowledgements

It goes without saying that there would be no book without the support of an astonishing amount of people. I can't even believe I finished this thing. It wasn't easy, and it took way longer than I anticipated. There's a story there and I will certainly tell it in due time but until then, a few words of extreme appreciation.

First and foremost, to my boys — Wyatt and Elias. Every single thing I do is for you. You guys are my light. I love you more than you will ever know.

To my parents for being my relationship role models and for showing me how to appreciate them fully. Mom, you inspire me and Dad, even though you're not here to physically experience this moment, I know you're around me. I think of you every day and I miss you. I love you both with my whole heart.

To my friends and family — all of you — for the laughter, the tears, the talks, the experiences and all of the wonderful memories we've made along the way. Here's to a lot more memory making in our futures.

To Michele and Anne — it all started in Spain, this is entirely your fault. (MWUAH!)

To Kathy — for your make good choices advice early on in my parenting and for your grace in the wake of profound loss. I have a picture of you and Matty on my desk, it keeps me grounded, grateful and motivated.

To Suanne, my inspiration — I want to be half the writer you are when I grow up. Thank you for your guidance through this pain in the ass process and for our "working" weekends at the lake house.

To Aimee and Andi — I mean, what do you say to the two friends who have been with you through it all since we were 12? Thank you doesn't seem like enough. I hope you know how much I love and appreciate you.

To my Ladies of the Lake — Thank you for listening to all the stories and living this process with me. You are my home and my happy place. Our adventures have just begun!

To the internet for giving me a place to network and meet some of the most amazing people on the planet. If it wasn't for social media I wouldn't know any of the other kick ass women out there, working so hard to be heard and make their mark on the world. And I wouldn't have the opportunity to connect with so many supportive people. You all rock!

To my round one reader's — Adrian, Trish, Shanny, Maria, Piera, Chrissy, Julia, Erin, and Kathy — thank you for your shoulders, ears and eyes and for volunteering to review these words with open hearts and minds. I'm so grateful to have you all in my life.

To my incredible launch group — I mean, you guys really stepped up to the plate! Reading the advanced copy and spreading the word about this book to your people...it means the world to me that you are invested in this. I will not forget this act of kindness and I appreciate it so much.

To my clients — you've taught me so much and have changed me for the better. I'm proud of you and I appreciate you.

To my YELLERS — none of this would be possible without this community we've built. Your encouragement, engagement and support over the last few years has been my center. Thank you for everything from the bottom of my heart.

To my out of this world editor, Misti — I don't even know where to begin. You came into this project at a time when I was most fragile, guided me through the content like a total pro and turned this book into something better than I could've ever imagined. And now you're stuck with me forever. I love you. I'll start outlining book 2!

To Jenny for your artistic brilliance and to Chris and Cindy for bringing this book to life.

To anyone who has ever crossed my path with a comment, a like, a quick chat or an eye roll, thank you. You don't go unnoticed or unappreciated (including the snark!).

To the dreamers — keep believing, and keep working toward making them happen. Because they do. I'm proof of that.

And finally, to Will — you are the reason for everything good in my life. I am forever grateful to have you by my side. Thank you for your inspiration, your love, your support and your occasional criticism while I started this new venture and tried my damndest to keep it all together. I love you beyond measure.

CPSIA information can be obtained
at www.ICGtesting.com
Printed in the USA
BVHW041317201118
533634BV00013B/124/P

9 781732 857223